WillowBerry lane

Gorgeous Quilts
for gracious living

by Sonja Moen & Vicki Lynn Oehlke

Gorgeous Quilts
for gracious living

by Sonja Moen & Vicki Lynn Oehlke

Copyright © 2009 by Landauer Corporation
Quilt designs copyright © 2008 by Sonja Moen & Vicki Lynn Oehlke
This book was designed, produced, and published by Landauer Books
A division of Landauer Corporation
3100 NW 101st Street, Urbandale, IA 50322
800-557-2144; www.landauercorp.com

President/Publisher: Jeramy Lanigan Landauer
Vice President of Sales and Operations: Kitty Jacobson
Managing Editor: Jeri Simon
Art Director: Laurel Albright
Technical Editor: Rhonda Matus
Photography: Craig Anderson Photography

Library of Congress Control Number: 2008937244

This book is printed on acid-free paper.
Printed in United States
10 9 8 7 6 5 4 3 2 1

ISBN 13: 978-0-9800688-6-3
ISBN 10: 0-9800688-6-x

TABLE OF CONTENTS

Introduction 4
General Instructions 5
Using BerriAngles® 8

Cottage Charm

Cottage Charm Quilt 14
    & Pillows 28
Cottage Lacework Quilt . . .34
Cottage Redwork Runner . .40

Villa Garden

Villa Garden Quilt 76
    Pillows 84
    Square Cloth 94
Sunset Table Runner 96
Villa Sunset Quilt 102
Villa Breeze Quilt 110
    & Pillows 116
Villa Shower Curtain 124

Lakeside Cottage

Cottage Square Cloth 48
    Napkins 50
    Roundcloth 51
    Place Mats 52
    Chair Cozy 54
Cottage Picnic Throw
    & Pillows 60
Lakeside Villa Quilt 64

Introduction

Vicki Lynn and Sonja live in the peaceful atmosphere of lake country in Devils Lake, North Dakota, with their families and, of course, their pets. Both love the art of quilting and sharing their creativity with others. That is what Gorgeous Quilts for Gracious Living is all about. Within these pages, you will find not only patterns for "Gorgeous Quilts", but also ideas for decorating your home with the softness and inviting warmth only quilts can give. Your Master Suite (yes - even the shower) to the table settings on your porch or patio will come alive when quilts are added to the mix.

The fabrics used in all of the projects are WillowBerry Lane Collections, designed by Sonja and Vicki Lynn with Maywood Studio. You will see how the two collections, Cottage Romance and Full Sun, lend a different feeling to the same quilt design.

We want to thank our families for their encouragement, and all the "nuts and bolts", or shall we say, "needle and thread" people who helped bring our Gorgeous Quilts to life: Barb Simons, Jolene Miller, Sue LaFleur, Vonnie Erickstad, and Karen Boe.

Here's to doing what you love the most in life!

General Instructions

Layering

◆ Cut the backing and batting 4" to 6" larger than the finished quilt top.

◆ Lay backing wrong side up on a smooth flat surface. Secure the edges with tape. Center the batting over the backing. Smooth the batting out. Layer the quilt top in the center of the batting. Smooth the quilt top out.

◆ Baste with large running stitches or small safety pins every 3" to 4". Begin in the middle and work out to the edges.

Quilting

By Hand

◆ Using hand quilting thread, thread a quilting needle with an 18" length of thread. Tie a small knot at the end. Insert the needle through the quilt top and into batting about 1" from where you want to begin quilting. Bring the needle up at the beginning of the quilting line. Give the thread a gentle tug to pull the knot through the quilt top and down into the batting.

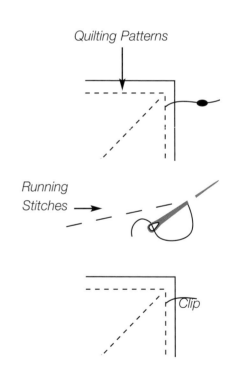

Quilting Patterns

Running Stitches

Clip

◆ Take several small running stitches at a time, keeping stitches even and as close together as possible (1/8" to 1/4").

◆ To end a line of stitching, make a small knot close to the fabric. Insert the needle into the fabric and bring it out again about 1" from the end of the stitching. Pop the knot through the quilt top into the batting and clip the thread close to the quilt top.

By Machine

◆ Use a walking foot for straight stitching of quilting lines. This will help to keep all layers of the quilt even. Pivot the fabric by keeping the needle in the down position when changing directions.

◆ Quilting stencils may be used for all types of designs. A free-motion or darning foot is used for this style of quilting.

General Instructions

BINDING

Double-fold (French-fold) Binding with Mitered Corners

1. To determine the length of binding needed for your quilt measure separately the length and width of the quilt and multiply each by two. Add these numbers together to get the total distance around the perimeter of your quilt. Add 16" to that number to cover the additional length needed for seams and corners. See the example for determining the binding length for a 60" x 80" quilt.

2. Divide the total length of binding by 40" (approximate fabric width, allowing for shrinkage) to determine the number of binding strips to cut for your quilt. See example for determining the number of binding strips needed.

3. Determine the finished binding width you would like for your quilt and multiply that number by four. Add 1/2" for seam allowances. See example for determining the width to cut your binding strips.

4. Cut the binding strips for your quilt from selvage to selvage. Sew the short ends of the binding strips, right sides together, with diagonal seams. Trim 1/4" from sewn line and press open. Fold the binding strips, wrong sides together, in half lengthwise, and press.

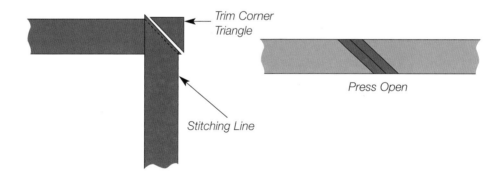

Trim Corner Triangle

Press Open

Stitching Line

5. Fold under a 1/2" hem at the beginning of the binding. Leaving approximately 4" of binding free, begin sewing the binding to the front of the quilt sandwich at the center on the bottom edge. Use a 1/4" seam allowance. Sew to 1/4" from the first corner, stop, and clip the threads. Remove the quilt sandwich from under the presser foot.

6. Fold the binding strip up at a 45-degree angle, as shown.

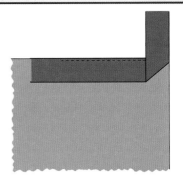

7. Fold the binding strip back down upon itself, making sure that the horizontal fold in the binding is even with the top edge of the quilt sandwich, as shown. Begin sewing the binding to the quilt exactly where the previous seam ended. Continue sewing and repeat steps 6 and 7 at each remaining corner.

8. To end, slide the end of the binding into the free portion at the beginning; sew the remaining seam.

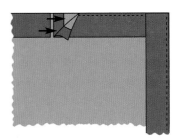

9. Bring the binding over the edge to the backing side of the quilt sandwich, and hand stitch in place. A folded miter will form at each corner; stitch these folds closed.

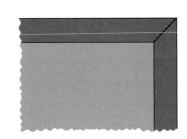

BIAS BINDING

1. Choose the fabric you will be using to bind your quilt and lay it out on a flat cutting surface. Find the 45-degree angle of your fabric with a ruler and cut binding strips the width needed. Join the binding strips together.

2. Leave 4" of binding free and beginning on an outer curve, sew the binding to the quilt sandwich as for double-fold binding. Do not stretch or pull the binding when sewing around the curves. Continue sewing the binding around the entire quilt sandwich.

3. End as for double-fold binding, sliding the end of the binding into the unsewn portion at the beginning. Bring the binding over the edge of the quilt sandwich and hand stitch in place.

Using Half-Square *BerriAngles*®

BerriAngles® are sewing notions designed to achieve accurate Folded Corner or Half-Square Triangles. The adhesive on the BerriAngles® holds the fabric layers securely in place, eliminating any shifting. Simply stitch on the dashed line and cut on the solid line and remove the BerriAngles®.

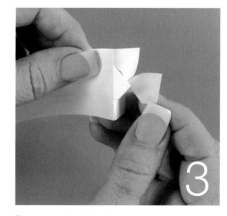

Determine the desired finished size of your Half-Square Triangle. The finished size is the measurement of the square once it is sewn into your quilt. Cut two fabric squares 7/8" larger than the desired finished size. For example, for a 2" finished Half-Square Triangle, cut two 2-7/8" squares of fabric. Each set of two fabric squares will result in two identical Half-Square Triangles.

Select a BerriAngles® size equal to the desired finished size of your Half-Square Triangle.

Remove the backing from the end tabs of the BerriAngles®; this is the area outside the V-shaped slits at each end of the BerriAngles®. Slightly fold each end tab to the back to open the slits.
Note: The only exposed adhesive is on the end tabs.

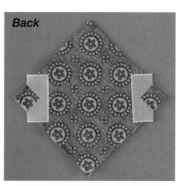

Back

Front

Press the adhesive side of the end tabs onto the back fabric square to secure the squares.

With right sides together, align the two same-size fabric squares. Treating the aligned fabric squares as one, insert one corner of the squares into one V-shaped slit. Insert the opposite corner into the remaining slit.

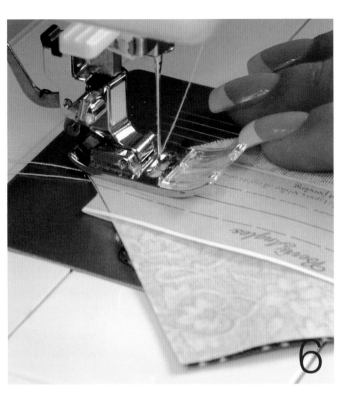

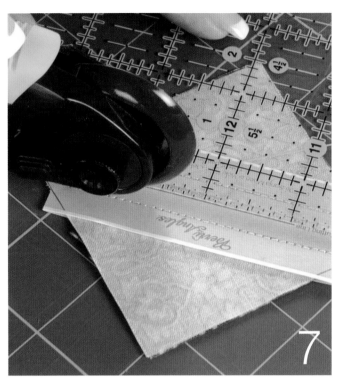

With the printed side of the BerriAngles® up, sew through all layers on each dashed stitching line.

Cut through the BerriAngles® and both fabric squares on the solid cutting line.

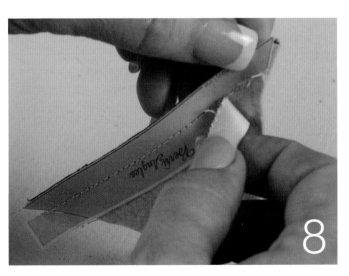

Open up the Half-Square Triangles and press the seam allowances open or toward the darker triangle.

Remove the BerriAngles® from the fabric squares. For easy removal, peel off the end tabs first and then tear off the larger portion of the BerriAngles® along the perforated stitching line as you hold the upper corner of the seam allowance.

Using Folded Corner *BerriAngles*®

Folded Corner BerriAngles® make it easy to construct perfect
snowball, flying geese, and square-in-a-square units.

1

Cut two sizes of fabric squares
as directed in your pattern. The
finished size of the squares will be
1/2" smaller once sewn in your quilt.

2

Select a BerriAngles® size that is
1/2" smaller than the cut size of
your small fabric square.

3

With right sides together, place the
small fabric square on one corner of
the large fabric square, carefully
aligning the edges.

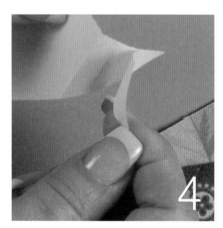

4

Remove the triangle-shaped
backing from each end of the
BerriAngles® to expose the adhesive
on the end tabs.

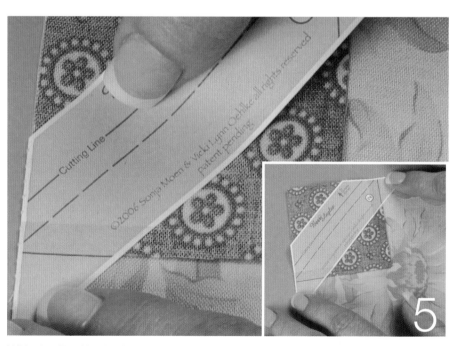

5

With the BerriAngles® printed side up, position it on the layered squares,
aligning the two short solid lines on the BerriAngles® with the inside edges of
the small square. The angled edges of the BerriAngles® and the edges of the
layered fabric squares should align. Press the adhesive side of the end tabs
onto the squares; it will adhere to both squares, securing them in place.

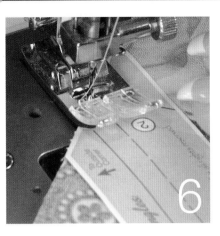

With the printed side of the BerriAngles® up, sew through all layers on the dashed stitching line.

Cut through the BerriAngles® and both fabric squares on the solid cutting line. Remove the BerriAngles® from the fabric squares. Fold, then tear the BerriAngles® along the perforated stitching line as you hold the upper corner of the seam allowance.

Open up the Folded Corner and press the seam allowances open or toward the triangle.

Adapting *BerriAngles®* for Different Sizes

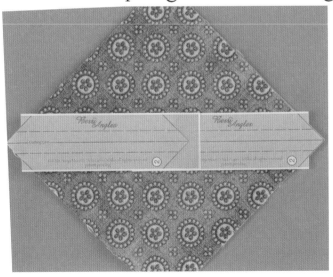

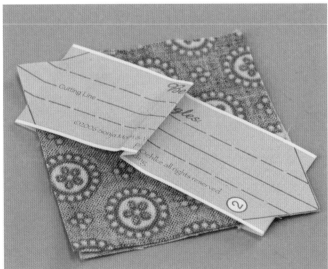

Piggy-Backing BerriAngles® is an option if you need a Half-Square (shown) or Folded Corner BerriAngles® larger than those available. Determine the diagonal of your fabric squares and overlap two or more BerriAngles® to achieve the length required. Remove the backing from the end tab of the top BerriAngles® and press the adhesive side to adhere to the overlapped BerriAngles®. Use this extended BerriAngles® in the same manner as instructed above.

Pinching BerriAngles® is an option if you need a Half-Square BerriAngles® smaller or in between the available sizes. Select a BerriAngles® size that is close to what you need. Insert the corners of the layered fabric squares into the V-shaped slits as directed on pages 8-9 in "Using Half-Square BerriAngles®". The excess length will arch above the squares. Simply pinch a crease near the center of the BerriAngles® to shorten it to the length needed. Finish the Half-Square Triangle in the same manner as instructed.

11

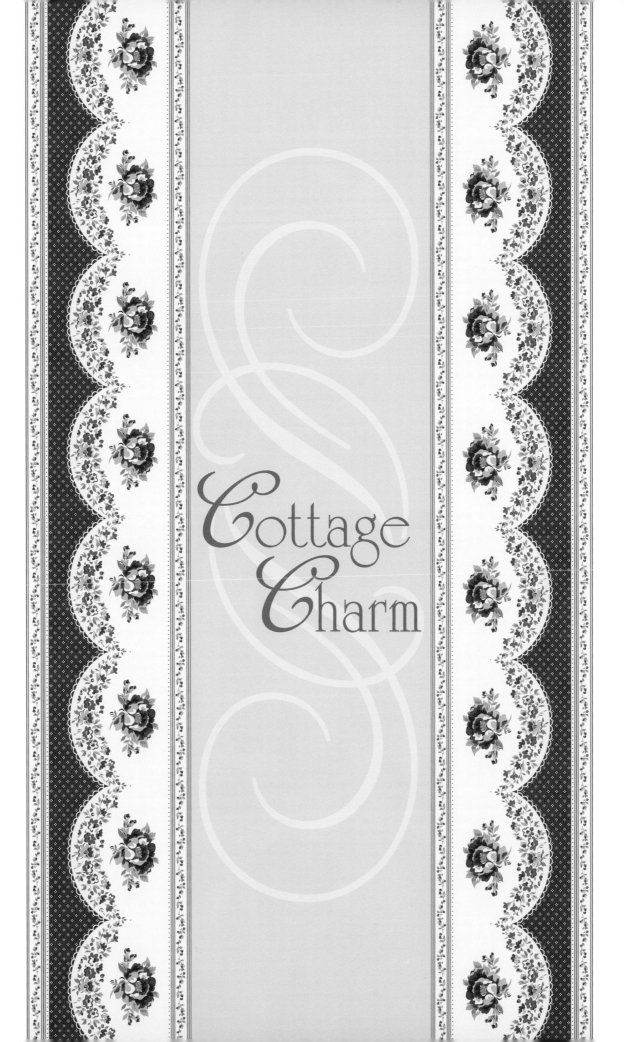

Cottage
Charm

Cottage Charm

The Cottage Charm quilt combines Ohio Star and Bird-In-Air blocks in a dramatic setting. Create your own queen-size masterpiece paired with coordinating shams.

Fabrics & Supplies

Finished size: 85" x 102"
Block size: Ohio Star, 9"; Bird-In-Air, 9"

A—2 yards ROSEBUDS
    Ohio Star Blocks, Pieced Triangles, Quilt Center,
    Borders, Quilt Top

B—1/2 yard SPRIGS ON WHITE
    Pieced Triangles, Quilt Center, Borders

C—3/4 yard RED SINGLE DOT
    All Blocks

D—1-1/4 yards RED SMALL FLORAL TEXTURE
    All Blocks, Pieced Triangles, Quilt Center, Borders

E—4 yards RED FLORAL RELIEF
    Bird-In-Air Blocks, Pieced Triangles, Quilt Center & Top

F—1/4 yard SKINNY RED STRIPE
    Quilt Center

G—1/2 yard RED DIAMOND DOT
    Bird-In-Air Blocks, Pieced Triangles

H—1/4 yard RED FLORAL STRIPE
    Borders

I—1/2 yard RED & WHITE CHECK
    Bird-In-Air Blocks and Pieced Triangles

J—1/4 yard RED WINDOWPANE
    Quilt Top

K—4 1/8 yards RED SCALLOP STRIPE
    Quilt Top

Backing—7-3/4 yards RED FLORAL RELIEF

Binding—1 yard RED FLORAL STRIPE

Batting—93" x 112" rectangle

Optional—Half-Square BerriAngles® (optional)
    52—2" Finished
    11—2-1/2" Finished
    14—3" Finished
    10—4" Finished

Before beginning this project,
see the General Instructions on pages 5-7.

Cutting Instructions

Ohio Star Block
Make 5 Blocks

Note: *If your Fabrics C and D measure at least 42-1/2" wide, you will only need to cut (1) 4-1/4" strip of each for the (C-1), (D-2) 4-1/4" squares.*

Fabric A ROSEBUDS:		
Cut (1) 3-1/2" x 40" strip.		
From the strip cut:		
(5) 3-1/2" squares		(A-1)
Fabric C RED SINGLE DOT:		
Cut (2) 4-1/4" x 40" strips.		(C-1)
Fabric D RED SMALL FLORAL TEXTURE:		
Cut (2) 3-1/2" x 40" strips.		
From the strips cut:		
(20) 3-1/2" squares		(D-1)
Cut (2) 4-1/4" x 40" strips.		(D-2)

Piecing the Ohio Star Block

1. With right sides together, layer the 4-1/4" x 40" RED SINGLE DOT (C-1) and RED SMALL FLORAL TEXTURE (D-2) strips in pairs for a total of two strip pairs; press. Cut the layered pairs into (10) 4-1/4" squares.

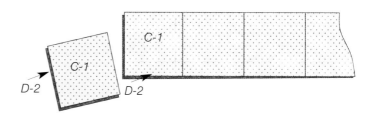

2. Keeping the above squares together in pairs, use a 4" Finished Half-Square BerriAngles® or draw a diagonal line across the wrong side of all the RED SINGLE DOT (C-1) squares. Stitch 1/4" on both sides of the drawn line. Cut apart on the drawn line; press seams toward dark triangles. The HALF-SQUARE TRIANGLES measure 3-7/8" square. Make 20.

Traditional Method

BerriAngles® Method

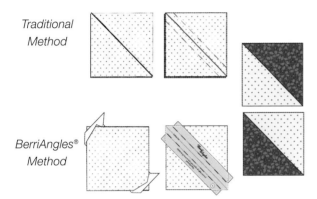

Note: See BerriAngles® pinching method on page 11.

3. Use a 3" Finished Half-Square BerriAngles® or draw a diagonal line on the wrong side of ten of the HALF-SQUARE TRIANGLES from Step 2. Layer the HALF-SQUARE TRIANGLES in pairs, aligning the seams and using one with a drawn line for each pair. Stitch 1/4" on both sides of the drawn line. Cut apart on the drawn line; press seams in one direction. The HOUR GLASS unit measures 3-1/2" square. Make 20.

4. Lay out four HOUR GLASS units, one 3-1/2" ROSEBUDS (A-1) square, and four 3-1/2" RED SMALL FLORAL TEXTURE (D-1) squares as shown.

5. Sew the pieces together in rows. Press the seam allowances away from the HOUR GLASS units. Sew the rows together; press. The Ohio Star Block measures 9-1/2" square. Make 5 blocks.

Cutting Instructions

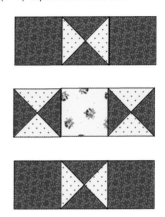

Bird-In-Air Blocks
Make 12 Blocks

Fabric C RED SINGLE DOT:
    Cut (4) 2-7/8" x 40" strips.   (C-2)
    Cut (1) 1-1/2" x 40" strip.
        From the strip cut:
        (12) 1-1/2" squares   (C-3)

Fabric D RED SMALL FLORAL TEXTURE:
    Cut (2) 4-1/2" x 40" strips.
        From the strips cut:
        (48) 1-1/2" x 4-1/2" sashing strips (D-3)

Fabric E RED FLORAL RELIEF:
    Cut (3) 2-1/2" x 40" strips.
        From the strips cut:
        (48) 2-1/2" squares   (E-1)

Fabric G RED DIAMOND DOT:
    Cut (3) 2-1/2" x 40" strips.
        From the strips cut:
        (48) 2-1/2" squares   (G-1)

Fabric I RED & WHITE CHECK:
    Cut (4) 2-7/8" x 40" strips.   (I-1)

Piecing Bird-In-Air Block

1. With right sides together, layer the 2-7/8" x 40" RED SINGLE DOT (C-2) and RED & WHITE CHECK (I-1) strips in pairs for a total of four strip pairs; press. Cut the layered pairs into (48) 2-7/8" squares.

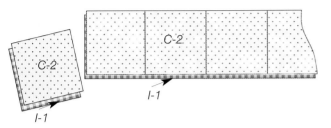

2. Keeping the above squares together in pairs, use a 2" Finished Half-Square BerriAngle® or draw a diagonal line across the wrong side of all the RED SINGLE DOT (C-2) squares. Stitch 1/4" on both sides of the drawn line. Cut apart on the drawn line; press seams toward dark triangles. The HALF-SQUARE TRIANGLES measure 2-1/2" square. Make 96.

Traditional Method

BerriAngles® Method

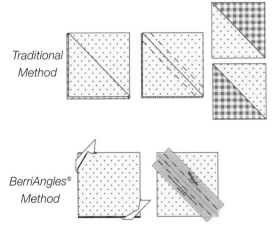

3. Arrange two HALF-SQUARE TRIANGLES from Step 2, one 2-1/2" RED DIAMOND DOT (G-1) square, and one 2-1/2" RED FLORAL RELIEF (E-1) square as shown. Sew the squares and half-square triangles together in pairs; press seams toward squares. Sew the pairs together; press. The BIRD-IN-AIR unit measures 4-1/2" square. Make 48.

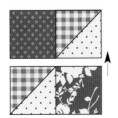

4. Layout four BIRD-IN-AIR units from Step 3, four RED SMALL FLORAL TEXTURE 1-1/2" x 4-1/2" (D-3) sashing strips, and one 1-1/2" RED SINGLE DOT (C-3) square as shown.

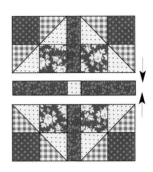

5. Sew the pieces together in rows. Press the seam allowances toward the sashing strips. Sew the rows together; press. The BIRD-IN-AIR block measures 9-1/2" square. Make 12 blocks.

Cutting Instructions

Pieced Triangle Unit
Make 11 Units

Fabric A ROSEBUDS: Cut (1) 5-1/2" x 40" strip. From the strip cut: (6) 5-1/2" squares; cut in half diagonally	(A-2)
Fabric B SPRIGS ON WHITE: Cut (2) 3-3/8" x 40" strips.	(B-1)
Fabric D RED SMALL FLORAL TEXTURE: Cut (2) 3" x 40" strips. From the strips cut: (22) 3" squares	(D-4)
Fabric E RED FLORAL RELIEF: Cut (8) 5-1/2" x 40" strips. From the strips cut: (22) 5-1/2" x 11-3/4" rectangles	(E-2)
Fabric G RED DIAMOND DOT: Cut (1) 3-3/8" x 40" strip.	(G-2)
Fabric I RED & WHITE CHECK: Cut (1) 3-3/8" x 40" strip.	(I-2)

Piecing the Triangle Unit

1. With right sides together, layer one 3-3/8" x 40" SPRIGS ON WHITE (B-1) with RED DIAMOND DOT (G-2) strip; press. Cut the layered pair into (4) 3-3/8" squares as shown. Layer the second SPRIGS ON WHITE (B-1) strip with the RED & WHITE CHECK (I-2) strip in the same manner. Cut (7) 3-3/8" squares from the layered pair.

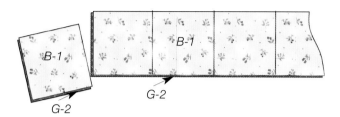

2. Keeping the above squares together in pairs, use a 2-1/2" Finished Half-Square BerriAngle® or draw a diagonal line across the wrong side of all the SPRIGS ON WHITE (B-1) squares. Stitch 1/4" on both sides of the drawn line. Cut apart on the drawn line; press seams toward dark triangles. The HALF-SQUARE TRIANGLES measure 3" square. Make 8 RED DIAMOND DOT and 14 RED & WHITE CHECK.

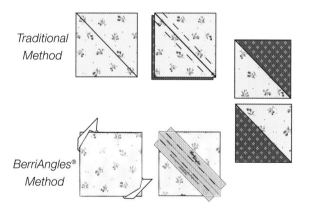

Traditional Method

BerriAngles® Method

3. Arrange two 3" RED SMALL FLORAL TEXTURE (D-4) squares and two RED DIAMOND DOT HALF-SQUARE TRIANGLES from Step 2 as shown. Sew the squares and half-square triangles together in pairs; press seams toward squares. Sew the pairs together; press. The BIRD-IN-AIR unit measures 5-1/2" square. Make 4.

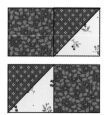

4. Arrange two 3" RED SMALL FLORAL TEXTURE (D-4) squares and two RED & WHITE CHECK HALF-SQUARE TRIANGLES from Step 2 as shown. Sew the squares and half-square triangles together in pairs; press seams toward squares. Sew the pairs together; press. The BIRD-IN-AIR unit measures 5-1/2" square. Make 7.

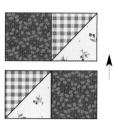

5. Sew one 5-1/2" x 11-3/4" RED FLORAL RELIEF (E-2) rectangle to the left edge of a ROSEBUDS (A-2) triangle. Sew a RED DIAMOND DOT BIRD-IN-AIR unit from Step 3 to the end of another RED FLORAL RELIEF (E-2) rectangle. Press seams toward rectangles. Sew the pieces together. Press seams toward triangle.

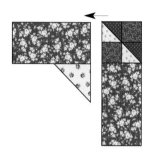

6. Use quilt ruler with a 45-degree marking and rotary cutter to trim ends of rectangles to align with triangle for one PIECED TRIANGLE UNIT. Repeat Steps 5 and 6 to make 4 units. Set aside for Quilt Center.

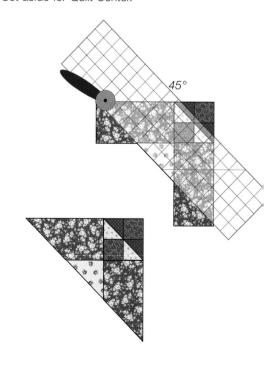

7. Using 7 RED & WHITE CHECK BIRD-IN-AIR units from Step 4 and 14 RED FLORAL RELIEF (E-2) rectangles, repeat Steps 5 and 6 to make 7 PIECED TRIANGLE UNITS as shown. Set aside for Pillow Tuck.

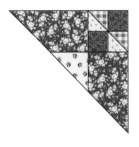

Quilt Center Cutting Instructions

Fabric A ROSEBUDS:	
Cut (2) 4-1/2" x 40" strips.	
From the strips cut:	
(4) 4-1/2" x 13-1/4" rectangles	(A-3)
Fabric B SPRIGS ON WHITE:	
Cut (1) 2-7/8" x 40" strip.	(B-2)
Fabric D RED SMALL FLORAL TEXTURE:	
Cut (1) 2-1/2" x 40" strip.	
From the strip cut:	
(8) 2-1/2" squares	(D-5)
Fabric E RED FLORAL RELIEF:	
Cut (1) 7-1/4" x 40" strip.	
From the strip cut:	
(2) 7-1/4" squares;	
cut each in half diagonally	
to make 4 triangles	(E-3)
Fabric F SKINNY RED STRIPE:	
Cut (1) 2-7/8" x 40" strip.	(F-1)

Piecing the Quilt Center

1. With right sides together, layer the 2-7/8" x 40" SPRIGS ON WHITE (B-2) and SKINNY RED STRIPE (F-1) strips; press. Cut the layered pair into (4) 2-7/8" squares.

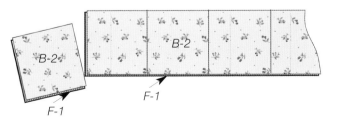

2. Keeping the above squares together in pairs, use a 2" Finished Half-Square BerriAngle® or draw a diagonal line across the wrong side of all the SPRIGS ON WHITE (B-2) squares. Stitch 1/4" on both sides of the drawn line. Cut apart on the drawn line; press seams toward dark triangles. The HALF-SQUARE TRIANGLES measure 2-1/2" square. Make 8.

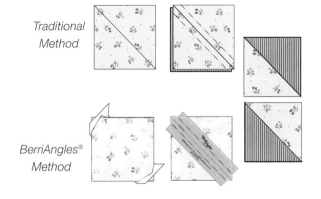

Traditional Method

BerriAngles® Method

3. Arrange two 2-1/2" RED SMALL FLORAL TEXTURE (D-5) squares and two HALF-SQUARE TRIANGLES from Step 2 as shown. Sew the squares and half-square triangles together in pairs; press seams toward squares. Sew the pairs together; press. The BIRD-IN-AIR unit measures 4-1/2" square. Make 4.

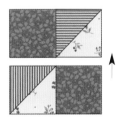

4. Sew two RED FLORAL RELIEF (E-3) triangles to opposite sides of one OHIO STAR block. Press seams toward triangles. Sew the remaining RED RELIEF FLORAL (E-3) triangles to the remaining edges of the block; press. The block unit should measure 13-1/4" square.

5. Sew two 4-1/2" x 13-1/4" ROSEBUDS (A-3) rectangles to opposite sides of the block/triangles unit from Step 4. Press seams toward rectangles.

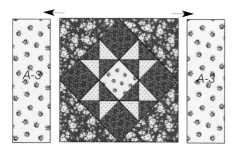

6. Sew a BIRD-IN-AIR unit from Step 3 to each end of the two remaining 4-1/2" x 13-1/4" ROSEBUDS (A-3) rectangles. Press seams toward rectangles. Sew these to the remaining edges of the block/triangles unit. Press seams toward rectangles.

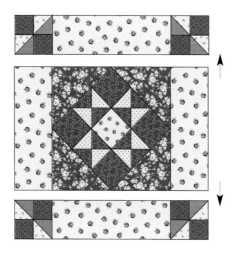

7. Sew two set aside RED DIAMOND DOT PIECED TRIANGLE UNITS to opposite sides of the quilt center. Press seams toward triangles units. Sew the remaining RED DIAMOND DOT PIECED TRIANGLE UNITS to the remaining edges of the quilt center; press seams away from center.

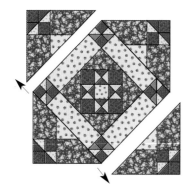

QUILT CENTER BORDERS
Cutting Instructions

Fabric A ROSEBUDS:
    Cut (5) 6-1/2" x 40" strips.
        From the strips cut:
        (4) 6-1/2" x 30" strips   (A-4)
        (8) 6-1/2" x 9-1/2" rectangles   (A-5)

Fabric B SPRIGS ON WHITE:
    Cut (1) 3-7/8" x 40" strip.   (B-3)

Fabric D RED SMALL FLORAL TEXTURE:
    Cut (1) 3-1/2" x 40" strip.
        From the strip cut:
        (8) 3-1/2" squares   (D-6)
    Cut (2) 1-3/4" x 40" strips.
        From the strips cut:
        (8) 1-3/4" x 9-1/2" sashing strips   (D-7)

Fabric H RED FLORAL STRIPE:
    Cut (1) 3-7/8" x 40" strip.   (H-1)

Adding First Border

1. With right sides together, layer 3-7/8" x 40" SPRIGS ON WHITE (B-3) and RED FLORAL STRIPE (H-1) strips; press. Cut the layered pair into (4) 3-7/8" squares as shown.

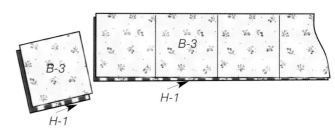

2. Keeping the above squares together in pairs, use a 3" Finished Half-Square BerriAngle® or draw a diagonal line across the wrong side of all the SPRIGS ON WHITE (B-3) squares. Stitch 1/4" on both sides of the drawn line. Cut apart on the drawn line; press seams toward dark triangles. The HALF-SQUARE TRIANGLES measure 3-1/2" square. Make 8.

Traditional Method

BerriAngles® Method

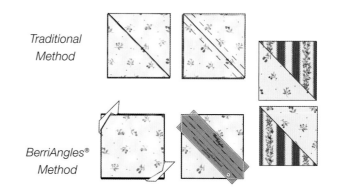

3. Arrange two 3-1/2" RED SMALL FLORAL TEXTURE (D-6) squares and two HALF-SQUARE TRIANGLES from Step 2 as shown. Sew the squares and half-square triangles together in pairs; press seams toward squares. Sew the pairs together; press. The BIRD-IN-AIR unit measures 6-1/2" square. Make 4.

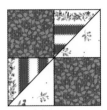

Make 4

4. Sew two 6-1/2" x 30" ROSEBUDS (A-4) rectangles to opposite sides of the quilt center. Press seams toward rectangles.

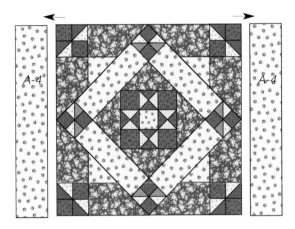

5. Sew a BIRD-IN-AIR unit from Step 3 to each end of the two remaining 6-1/2" x 30" ROSEBUDS (A-4) rectangles. Press seams toward rectangles. Sew these to the remaining edges of the quilt center. Press seams toward rectangles.

Adding Bird-In-Air Border

1. Join three BIRD-IN-AIR blocks with two 1-3/4" x 9-1/2" (D-7) sashing strips; press seams toward sashing strips. Add a 6-1/2" x 9-1/2" ROSEBUDS (A-5) rectangle to each end to make a border unit. Press seams toward rectangles. Make 4 border units.

2. Sew two border units from Step 1 to opposite sides of the quilt center. Press seams toward quilt center.

3. Sew an OHIO STAR BLOCK to each end of the two remaining border units. Press seams toward rectangles. Sew these to the remaining edges of the quilt center. Press seams toward center.

Quilt Top
Cutting Instructions

Fabric A ROSEBUDS:
Cut (2) 3-3/4" x 40" strips.
From the strips cut:
(12) 3-3/4" squares   (A-6)

Fabric E RED FLORAL RELIEF:
Cut (2) 30-1/4" x 40" strips.
From the strips cut:
(2) 30-1/4" squares;
cut each in half diagonally
to make 4 triangles   (E-4)
Cut (1) 3-3/4" x 40" strip.
From the strip cut:
(6) 3-3/4" squares   (E-5)

Fabric J RED WINDOWPANE:
Cut (1) 7-3/8" x 40" strip.
From the strip cut:
(3) 7-3/8" squares;
cut each in half diagonally
to make 6 triangles   (J-1)

Fabric K SCALLOP STRIPE:
Cut (8) 7" x 37"
lengthwise strips as shown.   (K-1)

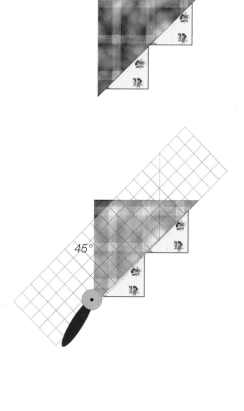

7"

7"

7"

7"

37"

Piecing the Quilt Top

1. Sew a 3-3/4" ROSEBUDS (A-6) square to one edge of a 3-3/4" RED FLORAL RELIEF (E-5) square. Press seams toward darker square. Sew another 3-3/4" ROSEBUDS (A-6) square to an adjacent side of the RED RELIEF FLORAL square to complete a unit. Press seams away from darker square. Make 6.

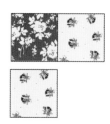

2. With right sides together, place a RED WINDOWPANE (J-1) triangle on each square unit as shown. Use quilt ruler with a 45-degree marking and rotary cutter to trim ROSEBUDS squares to align with triangle.

45°

3. Sew the triangle to trimmed square unit. Press seams toward triangle. The BIRD-IN-AIR unit measures 7" square. Make 6 units, 4 to use here for Quilt Top and 2 to set aside for Pillow Tuck.

4. Sew one 7" x 37" SCALLOP STRIPE (K-1) strip to one edge of a RED FLORAL RELIEF (E-4) triangle. Sew a BIRD-IN-AIR unit from Step 3 to the end of another SCALLOP STRIPE (K-1) strip. Press seams toward rectangle. Sew the pieces together. Press seams toward triangle.

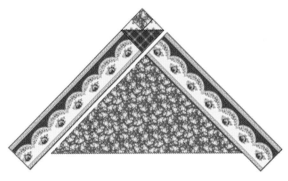

5. Use quilt ruler with a 45-degree marking and rotary cutter to trim ends of strips to align with triangle for one OUTER TRIANGLE UNIT. Repeat Steps 4 and 5 to make 4 units.

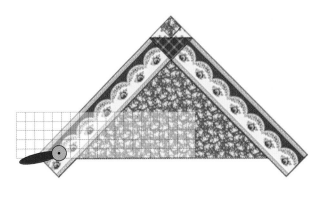

6. Sew two OUTER TRIANGLE UNITS to opposite sides of the quilt center. Press seams toward triangles units. Sew the remaining OUTER TRIANGLE UNITS to the remaining edges of the quilt center to complete the quilt top; press seams away from center.

Pillow Tuck

Cutting Instructions

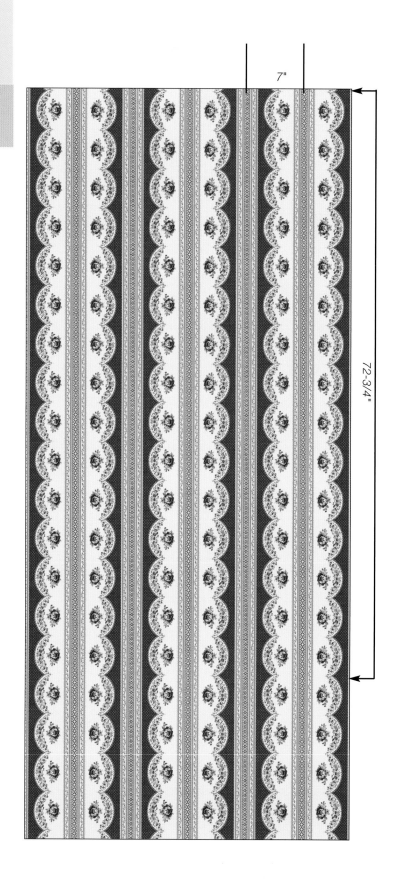

7"

72-3/4"

Adding Pillow Tuck

1. Lay out the 7 set aside PIECED TRIANGLE UNITS and 2 RED FLORAL RELIEF (E-6) triangles on a large flat surface as shown. Sew the units together; press seams in one direction. Add the RED FLORAL RELIEF (E-6) triangles to the ends; press seams toward triangles.

2. Sew a set aside BIRD-IN-AIR UNIT to the left end of the SCALLOP STRIPE (K-2) strip, positioning as shown. Press seam toward strip.

3. Sew the remaining BIRD-IN-AIR UNIT to the right end, positioning as shown. Press seam toward strip.

4. Sew the top border to the pieced triangle section to complete the Pillow Tuck. Press seam toward border. Sew the Pillow Tuck to the top edge of the Quilt Top. Press seam toward Quilt Top.

Finishing the Quilt
Cutting Instructions

Backing Fabric - RED FLORAL RELIEF:
Cut (3) 93" x Full Width of Fabric rectangles.

Binding Fabric - RED FLORAL STRIPE:
Cut enough 2-1/4" wide bias strips to make a 410" long strip.

1. Trim the selvages from the edges of the three backing rectangles. Sew the long edges of the rectangles together, using a 1/2" seam allowance. Press the seams open.

2. Layer the pieced backing, batting, and quilt top. Baste the layers together and machine- or hand-quilt as desired. See page 5 in the General Instructions for more information.

3. Prepare the binding and sew to the quilt front using a 1/4" seam allowance. Fold the binding to the back to cover the machine stitching and slip-stitch in place. See Bias Binding on page 7 for complete directions.

Cottage Charm

Cottage Pillows

Euro Sham

Fabrics & Supplies

Finished Size: 38" x 38"

A—1-1/4 yards ROSEBUDS
  Front

B—1 yard WINDOW PANE
  Front

C—1/3 yard SMALL FLORAL TEXTURE
  Inner Border

D—1 yard SCALLOP STRIPE
  Outer Border

Front backing—1-1/4 yards ROSEBUDS

Sham back—3 yards WINDOWPANE

Binding—3/4 yard FLORAL STRIPE

Batting—45" square

Before beginning project,
see General Instructions on pages 5-7.

Cutting Instructions
Cottage Euro Sham Front

Fabric A ROSEBUDS:
  Cut (1) 13-1/2" x 40" strip.
    From the strip cut:
    (2) 13-1/2" squares; cut squares in
    half diagonally to make 4 triangles (A-1)
    (2) 6-1/8" squares   (A-2)

Fabric B WINDOWPANE:
  Cut (1) 18-3/4" x 40" strip.
    From the strip cut:
    (1) 18-3/4" square   (B-1)
    (2) 6-1/8" squares   (B-2)

Fabric C SMALL FLORAL TEXTURE:
  Cut (4) 1" x 40" strips.
    From the strips cut:
    (2) 1" x 26-1/2" strips   (C-1)
    (2) 1" x 28" strips   (C-2)

Fabric D SCALLOP STRIPE:
  Cut (4) 5-1/2" x 28" lengthwise strips,
    centering a scallop in each strip as shown. (D-1)

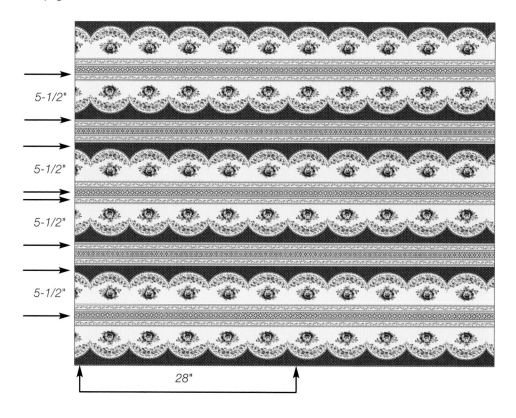

5-1/2"

5-1/2"

5-1/2"

5-1/2"

28"

Piecing the Euro Sham

1. Sew two ROSEBUDS (A-1) triangles to opposite sides of the 18-3/4" WINDOWPANE (B-1) square. Press seams toward the triangles. Repeat for the remaining sides to complete the sham center.

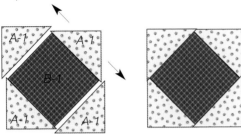

2. Sew the 1" x 26-1/2" SMALL FLORAL TEXTURE (C-1) inner border strips to opposite sides of the sham center. Press seams toward the strips. Sew the 1" x 28" SMALL FLORAL TEXTURE (C-2) inner border strips to the remaining sides of the sham center. Press toward the strips.

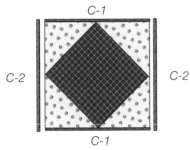

3. Draw a diagonal line across the wrong side of both 6-1/8" ROSEBUDS (A-2) squares. With right sides together, layer one ROSEBUDS (A-2) square on a 6-1/8" WINDOWPANE (B-2) square. Sew 1/4" on both sides of the drawn line. Cut apart on the drawn line; press toward dark fabric. The HALF-SQUARE TRIANGLES measures 5-1/2" square. Make four HALF-SQUARE TRIANGLE units.

Make 4

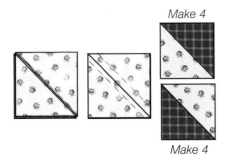

Make 4

Note: *Piggy Backing BerriAngles® is an option for this step. See page 11.*

4. Sew two 5-1/2" x 28" SCALLOP STRIPE (D-1) outer border strips to opposite sides of the sham center. Press seams toward the strips.

5. Sew a HALF-SQUARE TRIANGLE unit (made in Step 3) to each end of the remaining 5-1/2" x 28" SCALLOP STRIPE (D-1) outer border strips. Press seams toward the strips. Sew these to the two remaining sides of the sham center. Press seams toward the strips.

Finishing the Euro Sham Cutting Instructions

Fabric B WINDOWPANE:
   Cut (2) 42" x 38" rectangles.   (B-3)

Binding FLORAL STRIPE:
   Cut enough 2-1/2"-wide bias strips to make 170" long strip.

1. Layer the ROSEBUDS backing fabric, batting, and sham front. Baste the layers together and machine- or hand-quilt as desired. See page 5 in the General Instructions for more information.

2. Trim any excess batting and backing even with the raw edge of the pieced sham front, allowing for a 1/4" seam allowance.

3. Fold each of the 42" x 38" WINDOWPANE (B-3) rectangles in half with wrong sides facing, aligning the 38" edges opposite the fold; press. The back rectangles measure 21" x 38".

4. Smooth the quilted sham front, right side down, on a flat surface. Position a back rectangle on one half of the front, aligning three edges with the fold near the center. Position the second back rectangle over the remaining half of the front in the same manner. The rectangles will overlap approximately 4". Baste the layers together 1/4" from the raw edges.

5. To create the flange, sew through all layers, stitching-in-the-ditch on the seam that joins the SCALLOP STRIPE outer border to the SMALL FLORAL TEXTURE inner border.

6. Prepare the binding and sew to the sham front using a 1/4" seam allowance. Fold the binding to the back to cover the machine stitching and slip-stitch in place.

Standard Sham

Fabrics & Supplies

Finished Size:
39-1/2" x 30-1/2"

Note: *Yardage and Cutting Instructions are for two shams. Repeat sewing instructions to make a second sham.*

A—1-1/2 yards ROSEBUDS
    Sham Center

B—1/3 yard SMALL FLORAL TEXTURE
    Sham Center

C—1 yard FLORAL STRIPE
    Sham Center

D—1-1/2 yards RELIEF FLORAL
    Border

Backing—2 yards ROSEBUDS

Sham back—5-1/4 yards RELIEF FLORAL

Binding—7/8 yard FLORAL STRIPE

Batting—(2) 44" x 35" rectangles

Before beginning this project,
see General Instructions on page 5-7.

Cutting Instructions
Cottage Standard Sham Front

Fabric A ROSEBUDS:
    Cut (2) 5-1/2" x 40" strips.
        From the strips cut:
        (8) 5-1/2" squares   (A-1)
    (2) 20-1/2" x 40" strips.
        From the strips cut:
        (4) 12-1/2" x 20-1/2" rectangles   (A-2)

Fabric B SMALL FLORAL TEXTURE:
    Cut (3) 3" x 40" strips.
        From the strips cut:
        (32) 3" squares   (B-1)

Fabric C FLORAL STRIPE:
    Cut (4) 6-1/2" x 40" strips.
        From the strips cut:
        (8) 6-1/2" x 20" rectangles   (C-1)

Fabric D RELIEF FLORAL:
    Cut (8) 5-1/2" x 40" strips.
        From the strips cut:
        (4) 5-1/2" x 29-1/2" border strips (D-1)
        (4) 5-1/2" x 30-1/2" border strips (D-2)

Piecing the Sham Front

1. Draw a diagonal line across the wrong side of (16) 3" SMALL FLORAL TEXTURE (B-1) squares. With right sides together, place 3" SMALL FLORAL TEXTURE squares on opposite corners of a 5-1/2" ROSEBUDS (A-1) square as diagrammed. Stitch on the drawn line. Press toward the outside corners. Trim away excess fabric. Repeat for the remaining corners to complete a SQUARE-IN-A-SQUARE unit that measures 5-1/2" square. Make four.

Note: *Piggy Backing BerriAngles® Folded Corners is an option for this step. See page 10-11.*

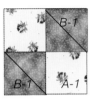 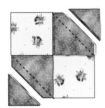

Make 4

2. Sew the four SQUARE-IN-A-SQUARE units together to make the center strip. Press seams in one direction.

3. With right sides together, fold a 6-1/2" x 20" FLORAL STRIPE (C-1) rectangle in half to align the long edges. Sew the long edges together, forming a tube. Turn the tube right side out. Press, centering the seam on the back. Make four.

Make 4

4. Mark the center of one long edge of two 12-1/2" x 20-1/2" ROSEBUDS (A-2) rectangles. Position two FLORAL STRIPE tubes from Step 3 on each ROSEBUDS rectangle so the tubes cross at the mark and the tubes are centered over the opposite corners as shown. Edge-stitch the tubes in place. Trim the tubes even with the edges of the ROSEBUDS rectangles to complete the side panels.

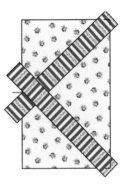 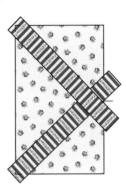

5. Sew a side panel to each long edge of the center strip for the sham center; press seams toward the side panels.

6. Sew a 5-1/2" x 29-1/2" RELIEF FLORAL (D-1) border strip to the top and bottom edges of the sham center. Press seams toward the strips. Sew a 5-1/2" x 30-1/2" RELIEF FLORAL (D-2) border strip to the remaining edges of the sham center. Press seams toward the strips.

Finishing the Sham
Cutting Instructions

Backing Fabric ROSEBUDS:
Cut (2) 44" x 35" backing rectangles.

Sham Back RELIEF FLORAL:
Cut (4) 43-1/2" x 30-1/2" rectangles.

Binding Fabric FLORAL STRIPE:
Cut enough 2-1/2"-wide bias strips
to make a 300" long strip.

1. Smooth a ROSEBUDS backing rectangle, right side
   down, on a flat surface. Center batting on backing rectangle and then the pieced sham front, right side up,
   on batting. Baste the layers together and machine- or
   hand-quilt as desired.

2. Trim any excess batting and backing even with the
   raw edge of the pieced sham front, allowing for a 1/4"
   seam allowance.

3. Fold two of the 43-1/2" x 30-1/2" RELIEF FLORAL rectangles in half with wrong sides facing, aligning the
   30-1/2" edges opposite the fold; press. The back rectangles measure 21-3/4" x 30-1/2".

4. Smooth the quilted sham front, right side down, on a flat
   surface. Position a back rectangle on one half of the front,
   aligning three edges with the fold near the center. Position
   the second back rectangle over the remaining half of the
   front in the same manner. The rectangles will overlap approx-

imately 4". Baste the layers together 1/4" from
the raw edges.

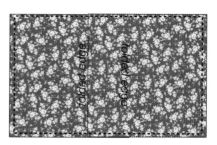

5. To create the flange, sew through all layers, stitching-in-the-
   ditch on the seam that joins the RELIEF FLORAL border to
   the sham center.

6. Prepare the binding and sew to the sham front using a 1/4"
   seam allowance. Fold the binding to the back to cover the
   machine stitching and slip-stitch in place. See Bias Binding
   on page 7 for complete directions.

Cottage Pillowcase

Fabrics & Supplies

Finished Size: Standard—21" x 32"; Queen—21" x 36"; King—21" x 42"

Note: *Yardage and Cutting Instructions are for two pillowcases in all sizes. Repeat sewing instructions to make a second pillowcase.*

A—2-1/2 yards ROSEBUDS

B—1/8 yard DIAMOND DOT

C—1-1/4 yards SCALLOP STRIPE

Before beginning project, see General Instructions on pages 5-7.

Cutting Instructions

Fabric A ROSEBUDS:
Cut (2) 28" x 43" rectangles for Standard; or
(2) 32" x 43" rectangles for Queen; or
(2) 38" x 43" rectangles for King.

Fabric B DIAMOND DOT:
Cut (2) 1-1/2" x 43" strips.

Fabric C SCALLOP STRIPE:
Cut (2) 12" x 43" lengthwise strips as shown. Each strip contains one full scallop and a partial scallop; cut the strip so the top edge is 1/2" beyond the red line at the top of the full scallop.

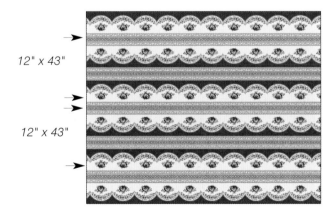

12" x 43"

12" x 43"

Sewing the Pillowcase

1. With right sides together, fold a 1-1/2" x 43" DIAMOND DOT strip in half lengthwise to measure 3/4" wide; press. Place the strip on the right side of a ROSEBUD rectangle, aligning the raw edges of the strip with a 43" edge of the rectangle.

2. Press under 1/2" on the partial-scallop edge of a 12" x 43" SCALLOP STRIPE strip. With right sides together, place the strip on the ROSEBUD rectangle, aligning the raw edges and sandwiching the DIAMOND DOT strip in between the layers. Sew the layers together with a 1/2" seam allowance. Press the SCALLOP STRIPE strip and the seam allowance away from the ROSEBUD rectangle.

3. With right sides together, fold the pillowcase in half, aligning the previous seam. Sew the end and the side together with a 1/2" seam allowance, leaving the SCALLOP STRIPE end open.

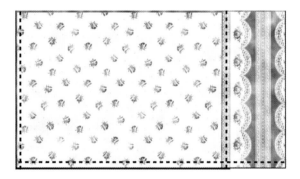

4. Fold the SCALLOP STRIPE strip in half, bringing the pressed edge to the seam line on the wrong side of the pillowcase; press. Turn the pillowcase right side out. Topstitch a scant 1/4" from the seam line, catching the pressed edge on the inside of the pillowcase in the stitching.

Cottage Lacework

This lovely red and white lap quilt speaks of elegance and simplicity. Lay the quilt at the end of your bed or toss it on your favorite chair. You will amaze yourself with your talent!

Fabrics & Supplies

Finished Size: 58" x 76" • Block Size: 13-1/2"

A—4-7/8 yards RED SINGLE DOT
      Blocks and Sashing

B—3-1/2 yards RED SMALL FLORAL TEXTURE
      Blocks and Sashing

Backing—3-5/8 yards ROSEBUDS

Binding—5/8 yard RED FLORAL RELIEF

Batting—64" x 82" rectangle

Optional —Folded Corner BerriAngles®
      240—1-1/2" Finished
      48—3" Finished

Before beginning this project,
see General Instructions on pages 5-7.

Cutting Instructions

Unit 1

Make 48 Units

Note: *If your fabrics measure at least 42" wide, you will only need to cut (7) 3-1/2"-wide strips from Fabric A for the 3-1/2" (A-1) squares and 3-1/2" x 2" (A-2) rectangles, (7) 2"-wide strips from Fabric B for the 2" (B-1) squares, and (4) 3-1/2"-wide Fabric B strips for the 3-1/2" (B-2) squares.*

Fabric A—RED SINGLE DOT:	
Cut (8) 3-1/2" x 40" strips.	
From the strips cut:	
(48) 3-1/2" squares	(A-1)
(48) 3-1/2" x 2" rectangles	(A-2)
Cut (3) 5" x 40" strips.	
From the strips cut:	
(48) 5" x 2" rectangles	(A-3)

Fabric B – RED SMALL FLORAL TEXTURE:	
Cut (8) 2" x 40" strips.	
From the strips cut:	
(144) 2" squares	(B-1)
Cut (5) 3-1/2" x 40" strips.	
From the strips cut:	
(48) 3-1/2" squares	(B-2)

Piecing Unit 1

1. Use 1-1/2" Finished Folded Corner BerriAngles® or draw a diagonal line across the wrong side of all 2" RED SMALL FLORAL TEXTURE (B-1) squares. With right sides together, place 2" RED SMALL FLORAL TEXTURE squares on opposite corners of a 3-1/2" RED SINGLE DOT (A-1) square as diagrammed. Stitch on the drawn lines. Press toward the outside corners. Trim away excess fabric if desired. Repeat with a third 2" square at one of the remaining corners. The pieced square measures 3-1/2". Make 48.

BerriAngles®
Method

Traditional
Method

Make 48

2. Sew together the pieced square (made in Step 1), one 3-1/2" x 2" RED SINGLE DOT (A-2) rectangle, and one 5" x 2" RED SINGLE DOT (A-3) rectangle as shown. Press seams toward the rectangles. The pieced square now measures 5". Make 48.

Make 48

3. Use 3" Finished Folded Corner BerriAngles® or draw a diagonal line across the wrong side of all 3-1/2" RED SMALL FLORAL TEXTURE (B-2) squares. With right sides together, place a 3-1/2" square on the corner of the pieced square from Step 2 as shown. Stitch on the drawn line. Press toward the outside corner. Trim away excess fabric. Unit 1 measures 5" square. Make 48 units.

BerriAngles®
Method

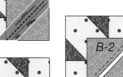

Traditional
Method

Make 48

Cutting Instructions
Unit 2
Make 48 Units

Note: *If your Fabric A measures at least 42" wide, you will only need to cut (7) 3-1/2"-wide strips for the 3-1/2" x 2" (A-4) rectangles.*

Fabric A RED SINGLE DOT:	
Cut (8) 3-1/2" x 40" strips.	
From the strips cut:	
(144) 3-1/2" x 2" rectangles	(A-4)
Cut (3) 5" x 40" strips.	
From the strips cut:	
(48) 5" x 2" rectangles	(A-5)
Fabric B RED SMALL FLORAL TEXTURE:	
Cut (5) 2" x 40" strips.	
From the strips cut:	
(96) 2" squares	(B-3)

Piecing Unit 2

1. Use 1-1/2" Finished Folded Corner BerriAngles® or draw a diagonal line across the wrong side of all 2" RED SMALL FLORAL TEXTURE (B-3) squares. With right sides together, place 2" RED SMALL FLORAL TEXTURE (B-3) squares on one end of two 3-1/2" x 2" RED SINGLE DOT (A-4) rectangles, orienting the lines in the direction shown to make one pair. Stitch on the drawn lines. Press toward the outside corners. Trim away excess fabric if desired. Repeat to make 48 pairs of pieced rectangles.

BerriAngles®
Method

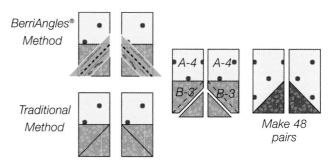

Traditional
Method

Make 48 pairs

2. Arrange one pair of pieced rectangles from Step 1, one 3-1/2" x 2" RED SINGLE DOT (A-4) rectangle, and one 5" x 2" RED SINGLE DOT (A-5) rectangle as shown. Sew the pieced rectangles together with the 3-1/2" x 2" rectangle; press seams toward the center rectangle. Add the 5" x 2" rectangle to complete Unit 2; press seam toward the rectangle. Unit 2 measures 5" square. Make 48 units.

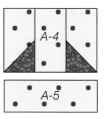

Make 48

Cutting Instructions
Unit 3
Make 32 Units

Fabric A RED SINGLE DOT:	
Cut (10) 2" x 40" strips.	(A-6)

Fabric B RED SMALL FLORAL TEXTURE:	
Cut (8) 2" x 40" strips.	(B-4)

Piecing Unit 3

1. Sew together the long edges of two 2" x 40" RED SMALL FLORAL TEXTURE (B-4) strips and one 2" x 40" RED SINGLE DOT (A-6) strip; press seams toward the dark fabric. The strip set measures 5" wide. Make four strip sets. Cut strip sets into (64) 2"-wide segments.

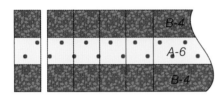

2. Sew together the long edges of two 2" x 40" RED SINGLE DOT (A-6) strips and one 2" x 40" RED SMALL FLORAL TEXTURE (B-4) strip; press seams toward dark fabric. The strip set measures 5" wide. Make two strip sets. Cut strip sets into (32) 2"-wide segments.

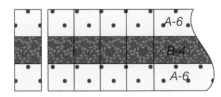

3. Position two segments from Step 1 and one segment from Step 2 as shown in the diagram. Sew the segments together to complete one Unit 3 that measures 5" square. Press seams away from the center segment. Make 32 units.

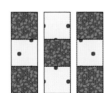

Make 32

Piecing the Lacework Block

Lay out four Unit 1, four Unit 2, and one Unit 3 as shown. Sew the units together in rows. Press the seams toward Unit 2. Sew the rows together; press. The block now measures 14" square. Make 12 Lacework Blocks. Set aside the remaining 20 Unit 3 for sashing.

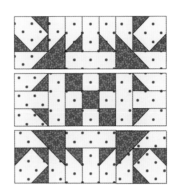

Make 12

Sashing
Cutting Instructions

Make 31 Sashing Strips

Note: *If your fabrics measure at least 42" wide, you will only need to cut (22) 2"-wide Fabric A strips and (11) 2"-wide Fabric B strips to make 11 strip sets.*

Fabric A RED SINGLE DOT:	
Cut (32) 2" x 40" strips.	(A-7)

Fabric B RED SMALL FLORAL TEXTURE:	
Cut (16) 2" x 40" strips.	(B-5)

Piecing the Sashing

Sew together the long edges of two 2" x 40" RED SINGLE DOT (A-7) strips and one 2" x 40" RED SMALL FLORAL TEXTURE (B-5) strip; press seams toward dark fabric. The strip set measures 5" wide. Make 16 strip sets. Cut strip sets into (31) 5" x 14" sashing strips.

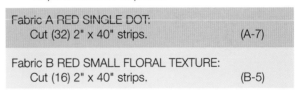

Quilt Top

1. Sew together four Unit 3 and three sashing strips as shown. Press seams toward the sashing strips. Repeat to make five sashing rows.

2. Sew together four sashing strips and three Lacework Blocks as shown. Press seams toward the sashing strips. Repeat to make four block rows.

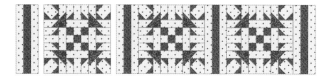

3. Sew together the sashing rows and block rows to complete the quilt top. Press the seams toward the sashing rows.

Finishing the Quilt
Cutting Instructions

Backing Fabric - ROSEBUDS:
    Cut (2) 65" x Full Width of Fabric rectangles

Binding Fabric – RED FLORAL RELIEF:
    Cut enough 2-1/4"-wide bias strips
    to make a 300" long strip.

1. Trim the selvages from the edges of the two backing rectangles. Sew the long edges of the rectangles together, using a 1/2" seam allowance. Press seams open.

2. Layer the pieced backing, batting, and quilt top. Baste the layers together and machine- or hand-quilt as desired. See page 5 in the General Instructions for more information.

3. Prepare the binding and sew to the quilt front using a 1/4" seam allowance. Fold the binding to the back to cover the machine stitching and slip-stitch in place. See Bias Binding on page 7 for complete directions.

Cottage Lacework

Cottage Redwork

Create this charming runner for your table. The red and white blocks appear very delicate and lacey but are easily put together. These blocks are enjoyable to piece, and go together quickly. It will also add charm and color to a dresser top.

Fabrics & Supplies

Finished Size: 26" x 64" • Block Size: 13-1/2"

A—1-7/8 yards RED SINGLE DOT
    All Blocks

B—1-5/8 yards RED SMALL FLORAL TEXTURE
    All Blocks

Backing—2 yards ROSEBUDS

Binding—1/2 yard RED FLORAL RELIEF

Batting—32" x 70" rectangle

Optional —Folded Corner BerriAngles®
    60—1-1/2" Finished
    12—3" Finished

Before beginning this project,
see General Instructions on pages 5-7.

Cutting Instructions

Unit 1
Make 12

Note: *If your Fabric B measures at least 42" wide, you will only need to cut (1) 3-1/2"-wide strip for the 3-1/2" (B-2) squares.*

Fabric A RED SINGLE DOT:	
Cut (2) 3-1/2" x 40" strips.	
From the strips cut:	
(12) 3-1/2" squares	(A-1)
(12) 3-1/2" x 2" rectangles	(A-2)
(1) 5" x 40" strip.	
From the strip cut:	
(12) 5" x 2" rectangles	(A-3)

Fabric B RED SMALL FLORAL TEXTURE:	
Cut (2) 2" x 40" strips.	
From the strips cut:	
(36) 2" squares	(B-1)
(2) 3-1/2" x 40" strips.	
From the strips cut:	
(12) 3-1/2" squares	(B-2)

Piecing Unit 1

1. Use 1-1/2" Finished Folded Corner BerriAngles® or draw a diagonal line across the wrong side of all 2" RED SMALL FLORAL TEXTURE (B-1) squares. With right sides together, place 2" RED SMALL FLORAL TEXTURE (B-1) squares on opposite corners of a 3-1/2" RED SINGLE DOT (A-1) square as diagrammed. Stitch on the drawn lines. Press toward the outside corners. Trim away excess fabric if desired. Repeat with a third 2" square at one of the remaining corners. The pieced square measures 3-1/2". Make 12.

BerriAngles®
Method

Traditional
Method

Make 12

2. Sew together the pieced square (made in Step 1), one 3-1/2" x 2" RED SINGLE DOT (A-2) rectangle, and one 5" x 2" RED SINGLE DOT (A-3) rectangle as shown. Press seams toward the rectangles. The pieced square now measures 5". Make 12.

Make 12

3. Use 3" Finished Folded Corner BerriAngles® or draw a diagonal line across the wrong side of all 3-1/2" RED SMALL FLORAL TEXTURE (B-2) squares. With right sides together, place a 3-1/2" square on the corner of the pieced square from Step 2 as shown. Stitch on the drawn line. Press toward the outside corner. Trim away excess fabric. Unit 1 measures 5" square. Make 12 units.

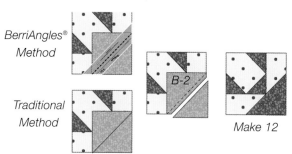

BerriAngles® Method

Traditional Method

Make 12

Cutting Instructions
Unit 2
Make 12

Fabric A RED SINGLE DOT:	
Cut (2) 3-1/2" x 40" strips.	
From the strips, cut:	
(36) 3-1/2" x 2" rectangles	(A-4)
(1) 5" x 40" strip.	
From the strip cut:	
(12) 5" x 2" rectangles	(A-5)
Fabric B RED SMALL FLORAL TEXTURE:	
Cut (2) 2" x 40" strips.	
From the strips cut:	
(24) 2" squares	(B-3)

Piecing Unit 2

1. Use 1-1/2" Finished Folded Corner BerriAngles® or draw a diagonal line across the wrong side of all 2" RED SMALL FLORAL TEXTURE (B-3) squares. With right sides together, place 2" RED SMALL FLORAL TEXTURE squares on one end of two 2-1/2" x 3" RED SINGLE DOT (A-4) rectangles, orienting the lines in the direction shown to

make one pair. Stitch on the drawn lines. Press toward the outside corners. Trim away excess fabric if desired. Repeat to make 12 pairs of pieced rectangles.

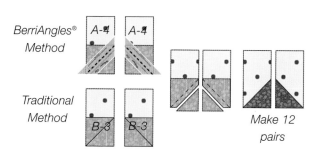

BerriAngles® Method

Traditional Method

Make 12 pairs

2. Arrange one pair of pieced rectangles from Step 1, one 3-1/2" x 2" RED SINGLE DOT (A-4) rectangle, and one 5" x 2" RED SINGLE DOT (A-5) rectangle as shown. Sew the pieced rectangles together with the 3-1/2" x 2" rectangle; press seams toward the rectangle. Add the 5" x 2" rectangle to complete Unit 2; press seam toward the rectangle. Unit 2 measures 5" square. Make 12 units.

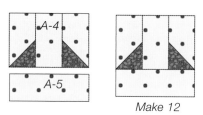

Make 12

Cutting Instructions
Unit 3
Make 11

Fabric A RED SINGLE DOT:	
Cut (5) 2" x 40" strips.	(A-6)
Fabric B RED SMALL FLORAL TEXTURE:	
Cut (4) 2" x 40" strips.	(B-4)

Piecing Unit 3

1. Sew together the long edges of two 2" x 40" RED SMALL FLORAL TEXTURE (B-4) strips and one 2" x 40" RED SINGLE DOT (A-6) strip; press seams toward the dark fabric. The strip set measures 5" wide. Make two strip sets. Cut strip sets into (22) 2"-wide segments

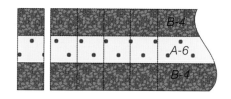

2. Sew together the long edges of two 2" x 40" RED SINGLE DOT (A-6) strips and one 2" x 40" RED SMALL FLORAL TEXTURE (B-4) strip; press seams toward dark fabric. The strip set measures 5" wide. Cut strip set into (11) 2"-wide segments.

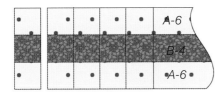

3. Position two segments from Step 1 and one segment from Step 2 as shown in the diagram. Sew the segments together to complete one Unit 3 that measures 5" square. Press seams away from the center segment. Make 11 units.

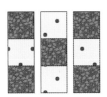

Make 11

Basic Block
Make 3

Lay out four Unit 1, four Unit 2, and one Unit 3 as shown. Sew the units together in rows. Press the seams toward Unit 2. Sew the rows together; press. The block now measures 14" square. Make 3 Basic Blocks. Set aside the remaining eight Unit 3 for later.

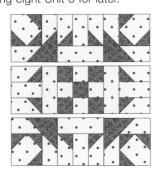

Make 3

Cutting Instructions
End Block
Make 2

Fabric A RED SINGLE DOT:
    Cut (2) 9-1/2" x 40" strips.
        From the strips cut:
            (12) 9-1/2" x 5" rectangles   (A-7)
      (1) 7-1/4" square; cut in half diagonally twice
          to make four triangles.   (A-8)
Note: *This will avoid having a bias on the*
    outside edge of the quilt.

Piecing the End Block

1. Sew together one 9-1/2" x 5" RED SINGLE DOT (A-7) rectangle and one Unit 3. Press seams toward the rectangle. Repeat to make six.

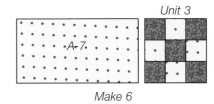

Make 6

2. Sew together one 9-1/2" x 5" RED SINGLE DOT (A-7) rectangle, one Unit 3, and one RED SINGLE DOT (A-8) triangle as shown. Press seams toward Unit 3. Make two.

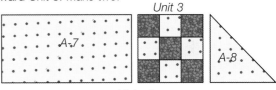

Make 2

3. Lay out one Basic Block, one A-7/Unit 3 from Step 1, and one A-7/Unit 3/A-8 from Step 2 as shown. Sew the block and pieced units together, pressing the seams away from the block. Repeat to make a second end block. Set aside the remaining A-7 and A-7/Unit 3 for later.

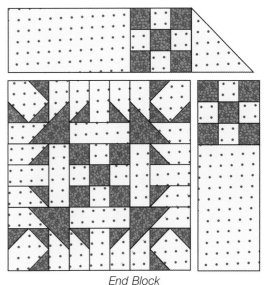

End Block
Make 2

Cutting Instructions

Triangles 1 and 2
Make 2 of each

Fabric B RED SMALL FLORAL TEXTURE:
   Cut (1) 14" x 40" strip.
      From the strip cut:
      (1) 14" square; cut in half diagonally twice
      to make four triangles   (B-5)
   (1) 7-1/4" x 40" strip.
      From the strip cut:
      (3) 7-1/4" squares; cut each in half diagonally
      twice to make twelve triangles   (B-6)
Note: *This will avoid having a bias on the outside edge of*
   the quilt.

Piecing the Triangles

1. Sew together one A-7/Unit 3 (made in End Block, Step 1)
   and one RED SMALL FLORAL TEXTURE triangle (B-6).
   Press seams toward the triangle. Make two.

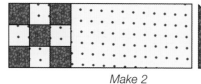

Make 2

2. Sew together one 9-1/2" x 5" RED SINGLE DOT (A-7)
   rectangle and one RED SMALL FLORAL TEXTURE (B-6)
   triangle. Press seams toward the rectangle. Repeat to
   make four.

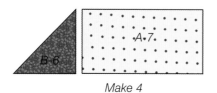

Make 4

3. Layout one RED SMALL FLORAL TEXTURE (B-5)
   triangle, one A-7/Unit 3/B-6 from Step 1, and one
   A-7/B-6 from Step 2 as shown. Sew the triangle and
   pieced units together to complete Triangle 1, pressing
   the seams away from the triangle. Repeat to make a
   second Triangle 1.

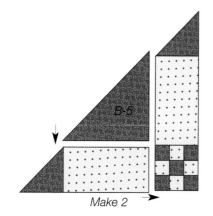

Make 2

4. Lay out one RED SMALL FLORAL TEXTURE (B-5)
   triangle, one A-7/Unit 3 (made in End Block, Step 1),
   and one A-7/B-6 from Step 2 as shown. Sew the
   triangle and pieced units together to complete Triangle 2,
   pressing the seams away from the triangle. Repeat to
   make a second Triangle 2.

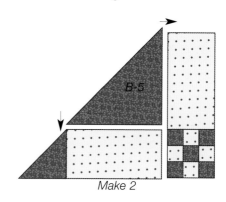

Make 2

Assembling the Runner Top

Lay out one Basic Block, two End Blocks, two
Triangle 1 and two Triangle 2 on a large flat surface as
shown. Sew the blocks and triangles together in rows.
Press seams away from the blocks. Sew together the
rows to complete the top. Press the seams in one
direction. The runner measures approximately 25" x 63".

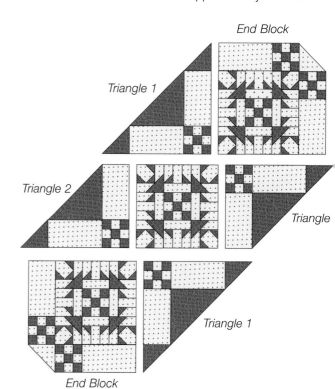

End Block

Triangle 1

Triangle 2

Triangle

Triangle 1

End Block

Finishing the Runner
Cutting Instructions

Backing Fabric - ROSEBUDS:
   Cut (1) 32" x 70" rectangle

Binding Fabric - RED FLORAL RELIEF:
   Cut enough 2-1/4"-wide bias strips
     to make a 210" long strip.

1. Layer the backing, batting, and runner top. Baste the layers together and machine- or hand-quilt as desired. See page 5 in the General Directions for more information.

2. Prepare the binding and sew to the quilt using a 1/4" seam allowance. See Bias Binding on page 7 for complete directions.

Cottage Redwork

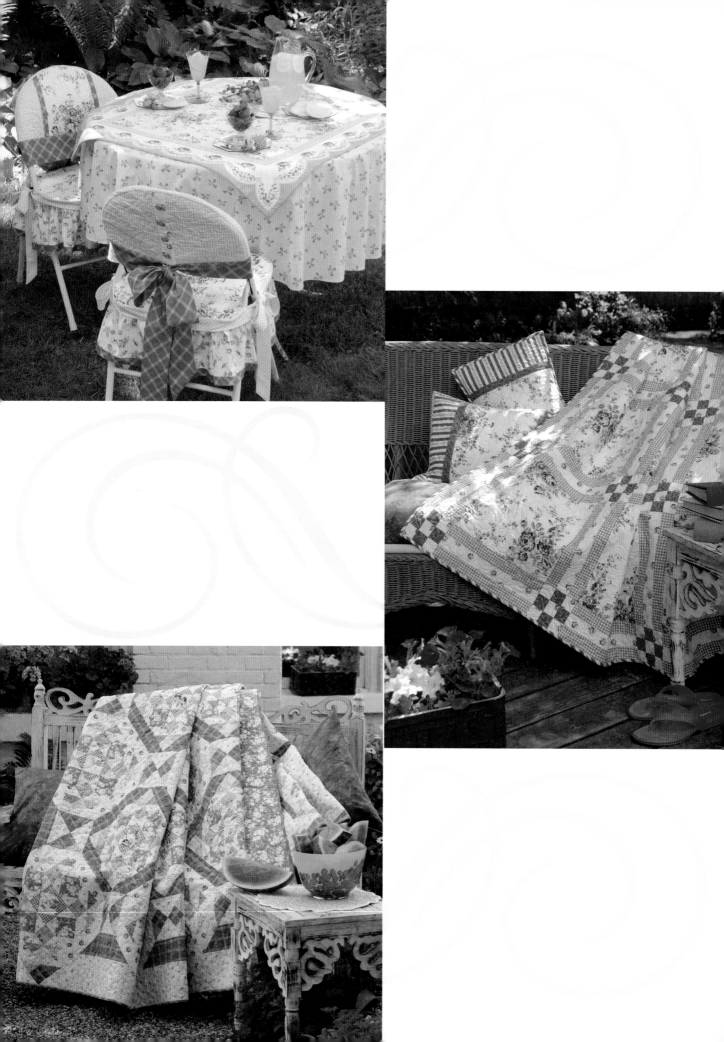

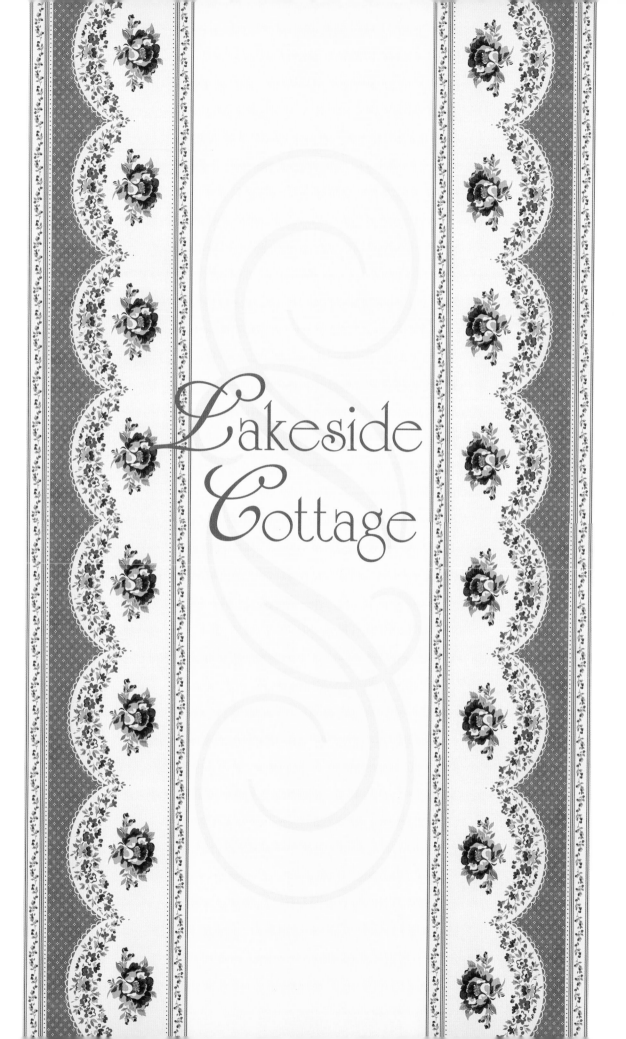

Lakeside Cottage

Cottage Square Cloth

Fabrics & Supplies

Finished Size: 38" x 38"

A—1-1/8 yards BOUQUETS – LARGE FLORAL
Front

B—1-1/8 yards TINY FLORAL
Back

C—2-3/8 yards SCALLOP STRIPE
Border

Batting—42" square

Before beginning project,
see General Instructions on pages 5-7.

Cutting Instructions

Fabric C SCALLOP STRIPE:
Cut (4) 12-1/2" x 40" lengthwise strips, centering a double scallop in each strip. Include eight full scallops in the length as shown.

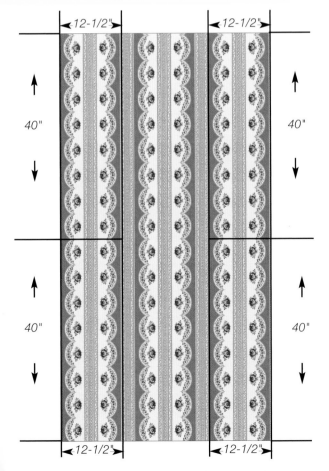

1. Remove selvages from Fabric A BOUQUETS – LARGE FLORAL and Fabric B TINY FLORAL.

2. Smooth Fabric B TINY FLORAL, right side down, on a flat surface. Center batting on Fabric B and then Fabric A BOUQUETS – LARGE FLORAL, right side up, on batting. Baste the layers together and machine- or hand-quilt as desired. Trim the quilted tablecloth to 38-1/2" square.

3. With wrong sides together, fold each 12-1/2" x 40" SCALLOP STRIPE border strip in half lengthwise to measure 6-1/4" wide; press.

4. Position a folded SCALLOP STRIPE border strip centered along one edge on the back of the tablecloth, aligning the raw edges. Sew the strip to the tablecloth with a 1/4" seam allowance, starting and stopping the stitching 1/4" from the adjacent edges of the tablecloth. Attach a SCALLOP STRIPE border strip to each edge of the tablecloth in the same manner.

Raw Edges of Folded Scallop

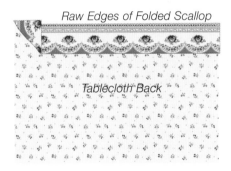

Tablecloth Back

5. To miter the corners, fold ends of SCALLOP STRIPE at 45-degree angles. Folds meet at the corner of the cloth as shown. Unfold one SCALLOP STRIPE to lay over the adjacent SCALLOP STRIPE. Draw a line from the inner corner where SCALLOP STRIPES meet to outer corner of the quilt body.

6. Fold tablecloth so quilt body is out of the way while you stitch the SCALLOP STRIPES together on the drawn lines. Trim seam allowance to 1/4". Press seams open. Repeat for each corner.

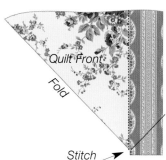

Quilt Front

Fold

Stitch →

7. Fold SCALLOP STRIPE border to the front of the tablecloth; press. Slip-stitch the inner folded border edge in place. If desired hand- or machine-quilt the border.

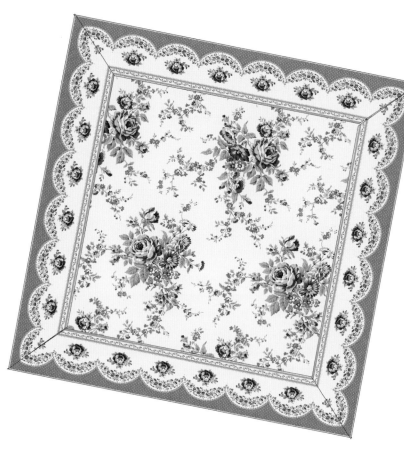

Cottage Napkin

Fabrics & Supplies

Finished Size: 20" square

Note: *Yardage and Cutting Instructions are for two napkins. Repeat sewing instructions to make a second napkin.*

A—5/8 yard BLUE RELIEF FLORAL
    Front

B—5/8 yard BLUE CHECK
    Back

C—1/2 yard MULTI SINGLE DOT
    Binding

Before beginning this project see
General Instructions on pages 5-7.

Cutting Instructions

Fabric A BLUE RELIEF FLORAL:
    Cut (2) 20" squares.

Fabric B BLUE CHECK:
    Cut (2) 20" squares.

Fabric C MULTI SINGLE DOT:
    Cut enough 2"-wide bias strips to
    make two 90" long strips.

1. With wrong sides together, layer a Fabric A BLUE RELIEF FLORAL square and a Fabric B BLUE CHECK square. Press with steam to hold the layers in place. Baste the layers together and machine- or hand-quilt to add texture and strength if desired.

2. Prepare the binding and sew to the napkin front using a 1/4" seam allowance. Fold the binding to the back to cover the machine stitching and slip-stitch in place. See Bias Binding on page 7 for complete directions.

Cottage Round Cloth

Fabrics & Supplies

Finished Size: 70" diameter

4 yards ROSEBUDS ON YELLOW

1-1/4-yards of string

Water-soluble marking pen

Before beginning project,
see General Instructions on pages 5-7.

Cutting Instructions

Fabric A ROSEBUDS ON YELLOW:
Cut (1) 72" x 44" center rectangle.
(2) 72" x 22" side rectangles.

1. Remove selvages from the rectangles. Sew each side rectangle to a long edge of the center rectangle with a 1/2" seam allowance. Press seams toward the center.

2. Fold the pieced fabric in half lengthwise, aligning the seams. Fold in half again crosswise, again aligning seams.

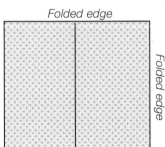

Folded edge

Folded edge

3. Tie one end of the string to a marking pen. Pin the other end to the folded corner of the fabric opposite the cut edges, keeping 35-1/2" between the fabric corner and the pen. With the string fully extended, draw an arc on the fabric. Cut through all four fabric layers on the marked line.

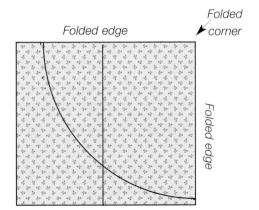

Folded edge

Folded corner

Folded edge

4. Sew 3/8" from edge of tablecloth. To hem, fold under 3/8" twice; press. Sew 1/4" from outer pressed edge.

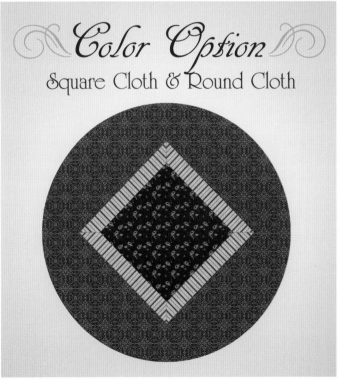

Color Option
Square Cloth & Round Cloth

Cottage Place Mat

Adorn your table with these delightful round scalloped place mats.

Fabrics & Supplies

Finished Size: 16" diameter

Note: *Yardage and Cutting Instructions are for two place mats. Repeat sewing instructions to make a second place mat.*

A—1/2 yard BLUE RELIEF FLORAL
   Front

B—1/2 yard BLUE CHECK
   Back

C—3/4 yard MULTI SINGLE DOT
   Binding

Batting—(2) 18" squares

Template plastic

Water-soluble marking pen

Before beginning this project see
General Instructions on pages 5-7.

Cutting Instructions

Fabric A BLUE RELIEF FLORAL:
   Cut (2) 18" squares.

Fabric B BLUE CHECK:
   Cut (2) 18" squares.

Fabric C MULTI SINGLE DOT:
   Cut enough 1-1/4"-wide bias strips
   to make two 75" long strips.

1. Smooth a Fabric B BLUE CHECK square, right side down, on a flat surface. Center batting on the BLUE CHECK square. Place a Fabric A BLUE RELIEF FLORAL square, right side up, on the batting. Baste the layers together and machine- or hand-quilt as desired.

2. Trace the SCALLOPED CIRCLE TEMPLATE on page 53 onto template plastic; cut out the shape. Mark the 18" quilted fabric square in four 9"-square quadrants as shown.

3. Place the template on the upper left quadrant of the quilted fabric. Use a water-soluble marking pen to draw along the scalloped edge of the template onto the quilted fabric. Reposition the template on each quadrant to complete the drawing. Cut on drawn line.

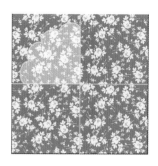

4. Working on the back of the place mat, use a water-soluble marking pen to make a dot 1/4" from each inside "V" of the scallops. To reinforce the corners, use a scant 1/4" seam allowance to sew about 1/2" on each side of every dot, pivoting at the dot. Clip through all layers of the place mat at the dots, cutting from the edge to the stitching line.

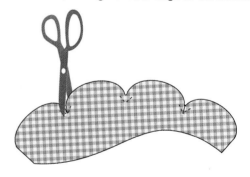

5. Pin a single layer of binding right side down on the place mat front, beginning and ending at an inside corner with a 4" tail at each end. To pin, insert a pin through a dot from the back of the place mat through the binding, then pin that location from the front. Remove the pin from the back. Pin binding around scallop to next dot. Continue around entire place mat in this manner. Sew binding to the place mat, stopping at each dot with the needle down. Pull gently at the clipped corner to straighten the seam, pivot the place mat, and sew to the next dot.

6. Fold the binding to the back of the place mat to cover the machine stitching, turning under the raw edge. Slip-stitch in place.

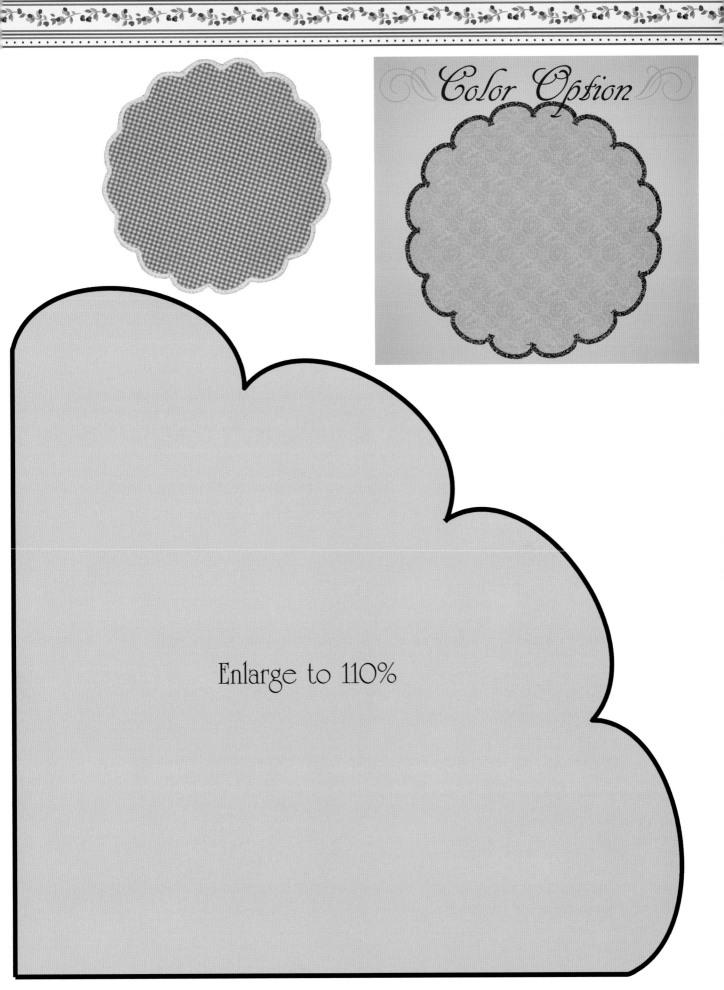

Color Option

Enlarge to 110%

Cottage Chair Cozy

Make adorable chair cozies for your folding chairs. They will dress up any occasion indoors or outdoors.

Fabrics & Supplies

Note: Fabrics, Supplies and Cutting Instructions are for two chair cozy sets. Repeat sewing instructions to make a second chair cozy set.

A—1 yard WHITE BOUQUETS
    Back and Seat Covers

B—3-1/2 yards RED WINDOWPANE PLAID
    Back Cover Trim and Tie and Skirt Trim

C—3 yards YELLOW & WHITE CHECK
    Back Cover and Seat Ties

D—1/4 yard ROSEBUDS
    Back Cover Trim

E—1-3/8 yards LEAFY ROSES
    Skirt

Backing—2 yards WHITE BOUQUETS

Batting—(4) 18" x 26" rectangles and (2) 18" squares

Freezer paper

Water-soluble marking pen

(8) 1-1/8" metal buttons to cover

4 yards 3/4" Velcro® Sew-On Loop Tape

4 yards 1" Velcro® Sticky-Back Hook Tape

Before beginning this project see General Instructions on pages 5-7.

Cutting Instructions

Fabric A WHITE BOUQUETS:
Cut (1) 8-1/2" x 40" strip.
    From the strip cut:
    (2) 8-1/2" x 14-1/2"
    center front rectangles   (A-1)
(1) 18" x 40" strip.
    From the strip cut:
    (2) 18" x 18" seat squares   (A-2)

Fabric B RED WINDOWPANE PLAID:
Cut (2) 2" x Width of Fabric
    bias strips for back trim .   (B-1)
(6) 8-1/2" x Width of Fabric
    bias strips for back tie .   (B-2)
Cut enough 2-1/2"-wide skirt
    trim bias strips to total 275".   (B-3)

Fabric C YELLOW & WHITE CHECK:
Cut (2) 14-1/2" x 40" strips.
    From the strips cut:
    (4) 14-1/2" x 7-1/2"
    side front rectangles   (C-1)
    (2) 14-1/2" x 10-1/2"
    left back rectangles   (C-2)
    (2) 14-1/2" x 12-1/2"
    right back rectangles   (C-3)
Cut (2) 1-1/2" x Width of Fabric
    bias strips for back gusset.   (C-4)
Cut enough 4"-wide seat tie bias strips
    to total 350".   (C-5)

Fabric D ROSEBUDS:
Cut (1) 3-1/2" x 40" strip.
    From the strip cut:
    (2) 3-1/2" x 14-1/2" back trim strips (D-1)

Fabric E LEAFY ROSES:
Cut (6) 7" x 40" skirt strips.   (E-1)

Backing Fabric WHITE BOUQUETS:
Cut (2) 26" x 40" strips.
    From the strips cut:
    (4) 18" x 26" chair back backing rectangles
(1) 18" x 40" strip.
    From the strip cut:
    (2) 18" chair seat backing squares

Piecing the Chair Back Cover
Front

1. Cut two 14-1/2"-long trim strips from the 2"-wide RED WINDOWPANE PLAID (B-1) bias strips. With wrong sides together, fold the 14-1/2" trim strips in half lengthwise to measure 1" wide; press. Place a trim strip on the right side of a 14-1/2" x 7-1/2" YELLOW & WHITE CHECK (C-1) side front rectangle, aligning the raw edges of the strip with a 14-1/2" edge of the rectangle. Baste in place. Repeat to make two.

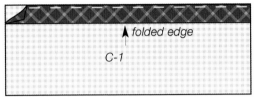

Make 2

2. Sew a side rectangle to each long edge of a 14-1/2" x 8-1/2" WHITE BOUQUETS (A-1) center front rectangle. Press seams toward the center.

Piecing the Chair Back Cover
Back

1. With wrong sides together, fold a 3-1/2" x 14-1/2" ROSEBUDS (D-1) strip in half lengthwise to measure 1-3/4" wide; press. Place the strip on the right side of a 14-1/2" x 12-1/2" YELLOW & WHITE CHECK (C-3) right back rectangle, aligning the raw edges of the strip with a 14-1/2" edge of the rectangle. Baste in place.

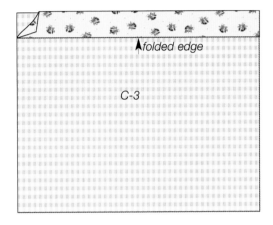

2. Sew together the right back rectangle and the 14-1/2" x 10-1/2" YELLOW & WHITE CHECK (C-2) left back rectangle. Press seam toward the left rectangle.

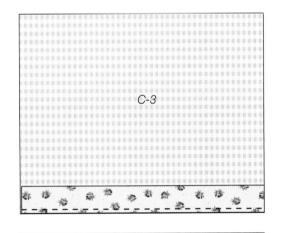

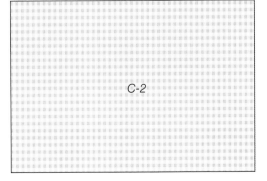

Finishing the Chair Back Cover

1. Smooth an 18" x 26" WHITE BOUQUETS backing rectangle, right side down, on a flat surface. Center an 18" x 26" piece of batting on the backing rectangle and then the pieced Chair Back Cover – Front, right side up, on the batting. Baste the layers together and machine- or hand-quilt as desired. Repeat with the pieced Chair Back Cover – Back and second rectangles of batting and backing.

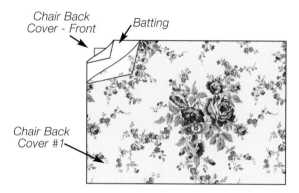

2. Trace the shape of your chair back onto the non-shiny side of a large piece of freezer paper, adding 1/4" seam allowances. Cut out the paper pattern. Position the pattern, shiny side down, onto the right side of the quilted Chair Back Cover – Front, taking care to center it over the center rectangle. Press; cut out the shape; gently peel off the paper pattern. Repeat for the Chair Back Cover – Back.

Chair Back Cover - Front

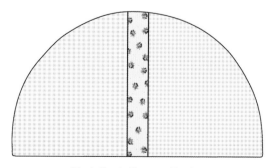

Chair Back Cover - Back

3. With right sides together, sew one 1-1/2"-wide YELLOW & WHITE CHECK (C-4) gusset bias strip to the curved edge of the Chair Back Cover – Back, leaving approximately 1" excess at the each end of strip.

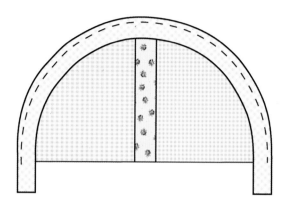

4. Sew the opposite edge of the 1-1/2"-wide YELLOW & WHITE CHECK (C-4) gusset bias strip to the curved edge of the Chair Back Cover – Front in the same manner. Trim the excess strip.

5. Turn Chair Back Cover right side out. Measure to find the circumference at the bottom edge of the cover. Use a water-soluble pen to mark the center front and the center back at the bottom edge of the cover.

Mark

6. Sew three 8-1/2"-wide RED WINDOWPANE PLAID (B-2) back tie bias strips together with diagonal seams to make one long tie strip; trim the strip to 147". With right sides together, fold the strip in half lengthwise to measure 4-1/4" wide. Use a water-soluble pen to make marks along raw edge at the strip center (to align with center front of quilted cover) and then on each side of the center mark at a distance equal to half the circumference found in Step 5 (to align with center back mark of quilted cover). Sew the tie's raw edges together with a 1/4" seam allowance, leaving an opening between the outer marks and stitching at a 45-degree angle at each end. Trim the ends and clip the seam allowance to the outer marks. Turn the tie right side out; press. Remark center on the right side of the tie.

7. Pin the tie to the bottom edge on right side of quilted cover, aligning the tie's center mark with the cover's center front mark and the tie's outer marks with the cover's center back mark. Sew the tie to the cover, backstitching as you begin and end the seam, removing pins as you sew. Press seam toward the tie.

8. To cover a button, place the 1-1/4" metal button on the wrong side of a 3"-square scrape of RED WINDOWPANE PLAID. Draw a circle about 1/2" beyond the edge of the button. Place button on a batting scrap. Draw around the button exactly at the button's edge. Cut out the fabric and batting circles on the lines. Center the batting circle on the wrong side of the fabric circle, then center the button on the batting. Refer to the package directions to complete the covered button. Make four covered buttons. Sew buttons evenly spaced on back trim of the chair back cover.

Batting Piece

Button

Batting

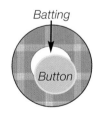

Button

Chair Seat Cover

1. Smooth an 18" WHITE BOUQUETS chair seat backing square, right side down, on a flat surface. Center an 18" square of batting on the backing rectangle and then an 18" WHITE BOUQUETS (A-2) seat square, right side up, on the batting. Baste the layers together and machine- or hand-quilt as desired.

2. Trace the shape of your chair seat onto the non-shiny side of a large piece of freezer paper, adding 1/4" seam allowances and marking the area where the folding legs cross the chair seat as shown. Cut out the paper pattern. Position the pattern, shiny side down, onto the right side of the quilted Chair Seat square. Press; cut out the shape; gently peel off the paper pattern. Transfer the markings to the quilted shape with a water-soluble marking pen.

3. Mark the center back of the quilted Chair Seat Cover with a water-soluble marking pen. Measure to find the distance between the back chair leg marks on the Chair Seat Cover.

4. Sew enough 4"-wide YELLOW & WHITE CHECK (C-5) seat tie bias strips together with diagonal seams to make one tie strip at least 160" long. Cut a 76" back tie; set aside remaining strip for Step 6. With right sides together, fold the strip in half lengthwise to measure 2" wide. Use water-soluble pen to make marks along raw edge at the strip center (to align with center back of quilted seat cover) and then on each side of center mark at a distance equal to half the distance found in Step 3 (to align with back chair leg marks). Sew the tie's raw edges together with a 1/4" seam allowance, leaving an opening between the outer marks and stitching at a 45-degree angle at each end. Trim the ends and clip seam allowance to outer marks.

Turn the tie right side out; press. Remark the center on the right side of tie.

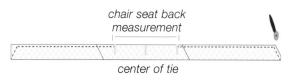

chair seat back
measurement

center of tie

5. Mark the center front of the quilted Chair Seat Cover with a water-soluble marking pen. Measure to find the distance between the front chair leg marks on the Chair Seat Cover.

6. Trim the set aside YELLOW & WHITE CHECK (C-5) seat tie strip to 84" for the front tie. With right sides together, fold the strip in half lengthwise to measure 2" wide. Use a water-soluble pen to make marks along raw edge at the strip center (to align with center front of quilted seat cover) and then on each side of center mark at a distance equal to half the distance found in Step 5 (to align with front chair leg marks). Sew the tie's raw edges together with a 1/4" seam allowance, leaving an opening between the outer marks and stitching at a 45-degree angle at each end. Trim the ends and clip seam allowance to outer marks. Turn tie right side out; press. Remark center on the right side of tie.

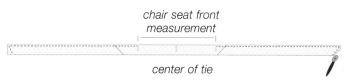

chair seat front
measurement

center of tie

7. Pin the front and back ties to the right side of quilted chair seat cover, aligning the ties' center marks with the cover's center front and back marks and the ties' outer marks with the cover's chair leg marks. Sew the ties to the cover, backstitching as you begin and end each seam. Remove the pins as you sew. Press seams toward the ties.

8. Clip the seam allowance to both chair leg marks on each side of the cover. Turn under 1/4" between the clips; stitch close to the folded edge in the chair leg areas.

Chair Skirt

1. Sew together enough 2-1/2"-wide RED WINDOWPANE PLAID (B-3) skirt trim bias strips with diagonal seams to total at least 125". With wrong sides together, fold the 2-1/2"-wide bias strips in half lengthwise to measure 1-1/4" for the skirt trim; press.

2. Sew together (3) 7" x 40" LEAFY ROSES (E-1) skirt strips to make one long strip. Align the raw edges of the trim strip from Step 1 with a long edge on the right side of the skirt strip. Sew the trim to the skirt strip; trim excess skirt trim. Press seam toward the skirt strip.

3. Apply 1" Velcro® Sticky-Back Hook Tape to the inside rim on the bottom of the chair seat. Follow the package directions for application. Measure the perimeter of the applied hook tape.

← back of chair seat

4. Starting and ending 1/4" from the short edges of the skirt, sew two rows of machine-basting 3/8" and 1/2" from the top edge of the skirt. Gently pull the basting threads on the right side of the skirt to gather the fabric to the measurement found in Step 3, plus 1/2". Anchor the threads at both ends by wrapping them around pins inserted in the fabric. Adjust the fabric to evenly distribute the gathers along the top edge. Sew the 3/4" Velcro® Sew-On Loop Tape to the right side of the skirt, centering it over the basting stitches and backstitching at the pins. Remove the pins; trim the basting thread.

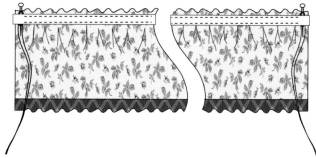

5. Sew together the short edges of the skirt with a 1/4" seam allowance to make a circle. Trim the loop tape close to the seam. Press seam open.

Dress the Chair

1. Slip the Chair Back Cover over the back of your chair. Tie the RED WINDOWPANE PLAID ties on the back of the cover.

2. Place the Chair Seat Cover on the top of your chair seat. Tie the YELLOW & WHITE CHECK ties at each side of the chair seat.

3. Attach the Chair Skirt on the underside of the chair seat by pressing the hook and loop tapes together.

Cottage Picnic Throw

Have a summer picnic with this adorable throw. Use it on your picnic table or spread it on the grass—it's washable. You may decide to use it on your front porch, thrown on a white wicker chair or sofa. Whatever you decide, you'll love making this easy, adorable quilt.

Fabrics & Supplies

Finished Size: 59" x 77"

Block Size: Plain, 13-1/2"; Nine-Patch, 4-1/2"

A—2-3/4 yards WHITE BOUQUETS
　　　Plain Blocks

B—1-1/4 yards ROSEBUDS
　　　Nine-Patch Blocks & Sashing

C—1/3 yard RED SMALL FLORAL TEXTURE
　　　Nine-Patch Blocks

D—2 yards BLUE & WHITE CHECK
　　　Sashing

E—3/4 yard RED FLORAL STRIPE
　　　Binding

F—3-5/8 yards backing fabric

Batting—65" x 83" rectangle

　　Before beginning project, see General Instructions on pages 5-7.

Cutting Instructions

Nine-Patch Block
Make 20 Blocks

Fabric B ROSEBUDS:
　　Cut (5) 2" x 40" strips.　　　　　(B-1)

Fabric C RED SMALL FLORAL TEXTURE:
　　Cut (4) 2" x 40" strips.　　　　　(C-1)

Piecing the Nine-Patch Block

1. Sew together the long edges of two 2" x 40" ROSEBUD (B-1) strips and one 2" x 40" RED SMALL FLORAL TEXTURE (C-1) strip; press seams toward dark fabric. The strip set measures 5" wide. Make two strip sets. Cut strip sets into (40) 2"-wide segments.

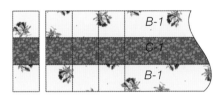

2. Sew together the long edges of two 2" x 40" RED SMALL FLORAL TEXTURE (C-1) strips and one 2" x 40" ROSEBUD (B-1) strip; press seams toward dark fabric. The strip set measures 5" wide. Cut strip set into (20) 2"-wide segments.

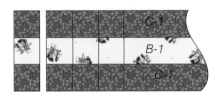

3. Position two segments from Step 1 and one segment from Step 2 as shown in the diagram. Sew the segments together to complete one Nine-Patch block that measures 5" square. Press seams toward the center segment. Make 20 Nine-Patch Blocks.

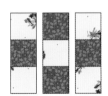

Make 20

Sashing
Make 31 Sashing Strips

Note: *If your fabrics measure at least 42" wide, you will only need to cut (11) 2"-wide ROSEBUDS strips and (22) 2"-wide BLUE CHECK strips to make 11 strip sets.*

Cutting Instructions

Fabric B ROSEBUDS:

    Cut (16) 2" x 40" strips.   (B-2)

Fabric D BLUE & WHITE CHECK:

    Cut (32) 2" x 40" strips.   (D-1)

Piecing the Sashing

Sew together the long edges of two 2" x 40" BLUE & WHITE CHECK (D-1) strips and one 2" x 40" ROSEBUD (B-2) strip; press seams toward dark fabric. The strip set measures 5" wide. Make 16 strip sets. Cut strip sets into (31) 5" x 14" sashing strips.

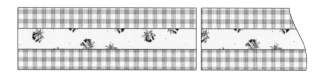

Quilt Top Cutting Instructions

Note: *If your fabric measures at least 42"-wide, you will only need to cut (4) 14"-wide WHITE BOUQUETS strips to make (12) 14" squares.*

Fabric A WHITE BOUQUETS

    Cut (6) 14" x 40" strips.

        From the strips cut:

        (12) 14" squares.   (A-1)

Piecing the Quilt Top

1. Sew together four Nine-Patch Blocks and three sashing strips as shown. Press seams toward the sashing strips. Repeat to make five sashing rows.

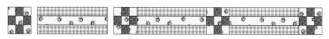

Make 5

2. Sew together four sashing strips and three 14" square WHITE BOUQUETS (A-1) blocks as shown. Press seams toward the sashing strips. Repeat to make four block rows.

Make 4

3. Sew together the sashing rows and block rows to complete the quilt top. Press the seams toward the sashing rows.

Finishing the Quilt Cutting Instructions

Fabric E RED FLORAL STRIPE:

    Cut enough 2-1/4"-wide bias strips to make a 300" long strip.

Fabric F Backing fabric:

    Cut (2) 65" x Full Width of Fabric rectangles

1. Trim the selvages from the edges of the two backing rectangles. Sew the long edges of the rectangles together, using a 1/2" seam allowance. Press seams open.

2. Layer the pieced backing, batting, and quilt top. Baste the layers together and machine- or hand-quilt as desired. See page 5 in the General Instructions for more information.

3. Prepare the binding and sew to the quilt using a 1/4" seam allowance. See Bias Binding on page 7 for complete directions.

Little Charmer Throw Pillow

You will adore this darling throw pillow. It is very easy to piece and will add charm to any room. Toss it on a chair or a window seat. Your guests will adore it too!

Fabrics & Supplies

Finished Size: 20" x 14"

A—1 yard WHITE BOUQUETS
 Front and Front Backing Rectangle

B—1/8 yard RED SMALL FLORAL TEXTURE
 Trim

C—1-1/2 yards RED FLORAL STRIPE
 Front, Back and Binding

Batting—24" x 18" rectangle

14" x 20" pillow form

 Before beginning project, see General Instructions on page 5-7.

Cutting Instructions

Fabric A WHITE BOUQUETS:
 Cut (1) 10-1/2" x 14-1/2
 center panel rectangle. (A-1)
 (1) 24" x 18" front backing rectangle. (A-2)

Fabric B RED SMALL FLORAL TEXTURE:
 Cut (1) 2-1/2" x 40" strip.
 From the strip cut:
 (2) 2-1/2" x 14-1/2" trim strips (B-1)

Fabric C RED FLORAL STRIPE:
 Cut (1) 5-1/2" x 40" strip.
 From the strip cut:
 (2) 5-1/2" x 14-1/2"
 side panel rectangles (C-1)
 (1) 24-1/2" x 40" strip.
 From the strip cut:
 (2) 24-1/2" x 14-1/2"
 back rectangles (C-2)
 Cut enough 2-3/8"-wide bias strips
 to make 80" long strip.

Piecing the Pillow Front

1. With right sides together, fold a 2-1/2" x 14-1/2" RED SMALL FLORAL TEXTURE (B-1) trim strip in half lengthwise to measure 1-1/4" wide; press. Place strip on the right side of a 14-1/2" x 5-1/2" RED FLORAL STRIPE (C-1) side panel rectangle, aligning the raw edges of the strip with a 14-1/2" edge of the rectangle. Baste in place. Make two.

2. Sew a side panel from Step 1 to each long edge of the 14-1/2" x 10-1/2" WHITE BOUQUETS (A-1) center panel rectangle with a 1/4" seam allowance. Press seams toward the center.

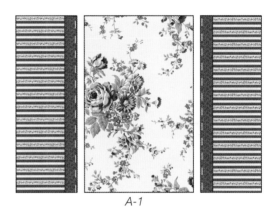

A-1

Finishing the Pillow

1. Smooth the 24" x 18" WHITE BOUQUETS (A-2) front backing rectangle, right side down, on a flat surface. Center batting on backing rectangle and then the pieced pillow front, right side up, on batting. Baste the layers together and machine- or hand-quilt as desired. Avoid catching the trim strips in the quilting.

2. Trim any excess batting and backing even with the raw edge of the pieced pillow front, allowing for a 1/4" seam allowance.

3. Fold the 14-1/2" x 24-1/2" RED FLORAL STRIPE (C-2) backing rectangles in half with wrong sides facing, aligning the 14-1/2" edges opposite the fold; press. The back rectangles measure 12-1/4" x 14-1/2".

4. Smooth the quilt pillow front, right side down, on a flat surface. Position a back rectangle on one half of the front, aligning three edges with the fold near the center. Position the second back rectangle over the remaining half of the front in the same manner. The rectangles will overlap approximately 4". Baste the layers together 1/4" from the raw edges.

5. Prepare the binding and sew to the pillow front using a 1/4" seam allowance. Fold the binding to the back to cover the machine stitching and slip-stitch in place. See Bias Binding on page 7 for complete directions. Insert pillow form in back opening.

Lakeside Villa

This Queen Quilt is wonderfully refreshing in blue and white with splashes of yellow. The three blocks that make up this quilt have identical center piecing with differences in the block borders. Blocks are set on point, along with pieced Setting Triangles.

Fabrics & Supplies

Finished Size: 90" x 108" • Block Size: 16"

A—6-1/2 yards WHITE SPRIGS
    All Blocks

B—1/2 yard each of FOUR GREEN PRINTS
    All Blocks

C—2-1/3 yards ROSEBUDS
    All Blocks

D—7/8 yard BLUE & WHITE CHECK
    All Blocks

E—5/8 yard YELLOW RELIEF FLORAL
    All Blocks

F—5/8 yard BLUE FLORAL ON PLAID
    All Blocks

G—2 yards BLUE RELIEF PRINT
    All Blocks

H—2/3 yard BOUQUETS ON WHITE
    All Blocks

I—2-3/4 yards BLUE WINDOWPANE
    All Blocks

Binding—1 yard BLUE WINDOWPANE

Backing—8 yards BLUE RELIEF FLORAL

Batting—96" x 114" rectangle

The Setting Triangle™

Optional—Half- Square BerriAngles®
    176—2" Finished

Optional—Folded Corner BerriAngles®
    560—2" Finished
    48—3" Finished
    48—1" Finished

NOTE: *See Piggy-Back Method in BerriAngles® Section.*

Before beginning project,
see General Instructions on pages 5-7.

Cutting Instructions

Basic Block
Make 28 Blocks

Fabric A WHITE SPRIGS:
    Cut (16) 2-7/8" x 40" strips   (A-1)
    (14) 2-1/2" x 40" strips.
        From the strips cut:
        (224) 2-1/2" squares.   (A-2)

Fabric B FOUR GREEN PRINTS:
    Cut (4) 2-7/8" x 40" strips
    from each to total 16 strips.   (B-1)

Fabric C ROSEBUDS:
    Cut (14) 2-1/2" x 40" strips.
        From the strips cut:
        (224) 2-1/2" squares.   (C-1)

Fabric D BLUE & WHITE CHECK:
    Cut (7) 2-1/2" x 40" strips.
        From the strips cut:
        (112) 2-1/2" squares.   (D-1)

Fabric E YELLOW RELIEF PRINT:
    Cut (7) 2-1/2" x 40" strips.
        From the strips cut:
        (112) 2-1/2" squares.   (E-1)

Fabric F BLUE FLORAL ON PLAID:
    Cut (7) 2-1/2" x 40" strips.
        From the strips cut:
        (112) 2-1/2" squares.   (F-1)

Fabric G BLUE RELIEF PRINT:
    Cut (14) 4-1/2" x 40" strips.
        From the strips cut:
        (112) 4-1/2" squares.   (G-1)

Fabric H BOUQUETS ON WHITE:
    Cut (4) 4-1/2" x 40" strips.
        From the strips cut:
        (28) 4-1/2" squares.   (H-1)

Piecing the Basic Block

Half-Square Triangle Units
Make 352

1. With right sides together, layer the 2-7/8" x 40" WHITE SPRIGS (A-1) and GREEN PRINTS (B-1) strips in pairs for a total of sixteen strip pairs; press. Cut the layered pairs into 2-7/8" squares, cutting (44) 2-7/8" squares from each of the four WHITE SPRIGS/GREEN PRINT fabric combinations.

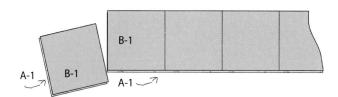

2. Keeping the above squares together in pairs, use a 2" finished Half-Square BerriAngles® or draw a diagonal line across the wrong side of all the GREEN PRINT (B-1) squares. Stitch 1/4" on both sides of the drawn line. Cut apart on the drawn line; press seams toward dark triangle. The HALF-SQUARE TRIANGLES measure 2-1/2" square. Make 88 HALF-SQUARE TRIANGLES from each GREEN PRINT for a total of 352 to be used for the BIRD-IN-AIR units and BLOCK 1.

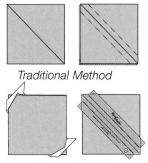

Traditional Method

Make 352

BerriAngles® Method

Bird-in-Air Units
Make 112

Arrange one 2-1/2" YELLOW RELIEF PRINT (E-1) square, one 2-1/2" BLUE FLORAL ON PLAID (F-1) square, and two HALF-SQUARE TRIANGLES with different greens (made in Step 1). Sew the squares and half-square triangles together in pairs; press seams

toward the squares. Sew the pairs together; press. The BIRD-IN-AIR unit measures 4-1/2" square. Make 112.

Make 112

Square-in-a-Square Units

WHITE CENTER
Make 28

Use 2" Finished Folded Corner BerriAngles® or draw a diagonal line across the wrong side of all 2-1/2" BLUE & WHITE CHECK (D-1) squares. With right sides together, place 2-1/2" BLUE & WHITE CHECK squares on opposite corners of a 4-1/2" BOUQUETS ON WHITE (H-1) square as diagrammed. Stitch on the drawn lines. Press toward the outside corners. Trim away excess fabric if desired. Repeat for the remaining corners. The SQUARE-IN-A-SQUARE unit measures 4-1/2" square. Make 28.

BerriAngles® Method

Traditional Method

Make 28

BLUE CENTER
Make 112

Use 2" Finished Folded Corner BerriAngles® or draw a diagonal line across the wrong side of all 2-1/2" WHITE SPRIGS (A-2) and ROSEBUDS (C-1) squares. With right sides together, place a 2-1/2" WHITE SPRIGS (A-2) square, on one corner of the 4-1/2" BLUE RELIEF FLORAL (G-1) square. Place a 2-1/2" ROSEBUDS (C-1) square on the opposite corner of the 4 1-/2" BLUE RELIEF FLORAL (G-1) square. Stitch on the drawn lines. Press toward the outside corners. Trim away excess fabric if desired. Repeat for the remaining corners. The SQUARE-IN-A-SQUARE unit measures 4-1/2" square. Make 112.

BerriAngles® Method

Traditional Method

Make 112

Joining the Units

1. Lay out four BIRD-IN-AIR units, four BLUE CENTER SQUARE-IN-A-SQUARE units, and one WHITE CENTER SQUARE-IN-A-SQUARE unit as shown. Make sure the BLUE CENTER SQUARE-IN-A-SQUARE units are placed with the WHITE SPRIGS fabric next to the BLUE CHECK fabric of the center Square-in-a-Square.

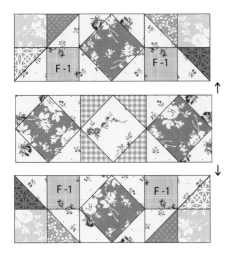

2. Sew the units together in rows. Press the seam allowances away from the BLUE CENTER SQUARE-IN-A-SQUARE units. Sew the rows together; press. The BASIC BLOCK measures 12-1/2" square.

    Note: *If your block does not measure 12-1/2" square, you may need to trim some of the units in future steps.*

Cutting Instructions
Block 1
Make 16 Blocks

Fabric C ROSEBUDS:
    Cut (16) 2-1/2" x 40" strips
        From the strips cut:
           (64) 2-1/2" x 8-1/2" rectangles   (C-2)

Fabric I BLUE WINDOW PANE:
    Cut (4) 2-1/2" x 40" strips
        From the strips cut:
           (64) 2-1/2" squares   (I-1)

Piecing Block 1
Half-Square Triangle/Rectangle Strip Units
Make 64

Position a HALF-SQUARE TRIANGLE unit (made in Step 1 of Piecing the Basic Block) at each end of a 2-1/2" x 8-1/2" ROSEBUDS (C-2) rectangle. Place the green triangles of the half-square units to mirror each other for the top outside corners of the sewn strips. Sew the

HALF-SQUARE TRIANGLE units to the rectangles; press seams toward the rectangles. Make 64.

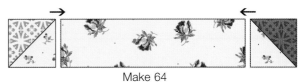

Make 64

Join Strip Units to Basic Blocks
Make 16

Note: *Only 32 strip units will be used in this step.*
    Position pieced strips from previous step on opposite sides of sixteen BASIC BLOCKS so the green triangles will again become the outside corners once sewn. Sew the strip units in place; press seams away from Basic Block. Make 16.

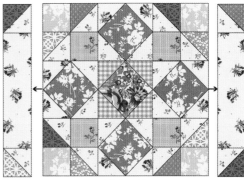

Make 16

Finish Block 1
Make 16

Sew a BLUE WINDOW PANE (I-1) square to each end of the remaining 32 pieced strips. Press seams away from the squares. Position these on the two remaining sides of the same 16 BASIC BLOCKS so the green triangles will be along the outside edge once sewn. Sew the pieced strip units in place. Press seams away from the Basic Block.

Make 16

Cutting Instructions

Block 2
Make 9 Blocks

Fabric A WHITE SPRIGS:
    Cut (5) 4-1/2" x 40" strips.
        From the strips cut:
        (36) 4-1/2" squares   (A-3)

Fabric I BLUE WINDOW PANE:
    Cut (15) 2-1/2" x 40" strips.
        From the strips cut:
        (18) 2-1/2" x 12-1/2" strips   (I-2)
        (18) 2-1/2" x 16-1/2" strips   (I-3)

Piecing Block 2

Blue Window Pane Border
Make 9

1. Trim the (18) 2-1/2" x 12-1/2" BLUE WINDOW PANE (I-2) strips to the BASIC BLOCK width, if needed. Sew these to opposite sides of nine BASIC BLOCKS; press toward the strips.

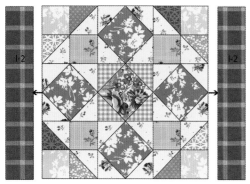

Make 9

2. Trim the (18) 2-1/2" x 16-1/2" BLUE WINDOW PANE (I-3) strips to the I-2/BASIC BLOCK width, if needed. Sew these to the remaining sides of the nine BASIC BLOCKS; press toward the strips.

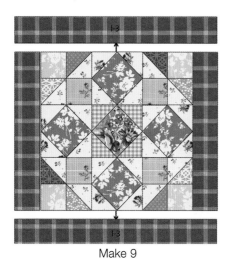

Make 9

Corner Triangles

Draw a diagonal line across the wrong side of the 4-1/2" WHITE SPRIGS (A-3) squares. With right sides together, place the 4-1/2" squares on each corner of the nine Block 2. Stitch on the drawn line. Press toward the outside corner. Trim away excess fabric. BLOCK 2 measures 16-1/2" square.

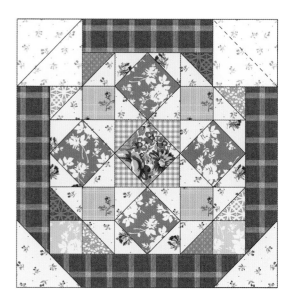

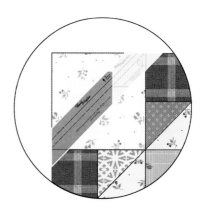

Note: *Piggy Backing BerriAngles® is an option for this step. See page 11 in the BerriAngles® Section.*

Cutting Instructions
Block 3
Make 3 Blocks

Fabric A WHITE SPRIGS:
    Cut (2) 4-1/2" x 40" strips.
        From the strips cut:
        (12) 4-1/2" squares   (A-3)

Fabric D BLUE & WHITE CHECK:
    Cut (3) 2-1/2" x 40" strips.
        From the strips, cut:
        (12) 2-1/2" squares   (D-2)
        (12) 2-1/2" x 4-1/2" rectangles   (D-3)

Fabric C ROSEBUDS:
    Cut (3) 1-1/2" x 40" strips.   (C-3)

Fabric I BLUE WINDOW PANE:
    Cut (3) 1-1/2" x 40" strips.   (I-4)

Piecing Block 3
Strip Set Border

Join the 1-1/2" x 40" ROSEBUDS (C-3) strips and
BLUE WINDOW PANE (I-4) strips in pairs with right
sides together to make strip sets. Press seams
toward the dark strips. Cut strip sets into twelve
2-1/2" x 8-1/2" segments.

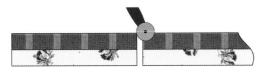

Add Blue & White Check

1. Sew a 2-1/2" BLUE & WHITE CHECK (D-2) square to each
   end of six STRIP SEGMENTS made in Step 1. Press
   toward the segments. Trim to the BASIC BLOCK
   width, if necessary. Sew these to opposite sides of the
   three remaining BASIC BLOCKS. Press seams away from
   the BASIC BLOCK.

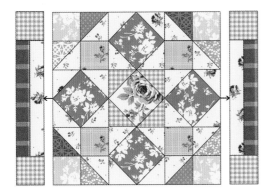

2. Sew one 2-1/2" x 4-1/2" BLUE & WHITE CHECK (D-3)
   rectangle to remaining strip segments; press toward the
   segments. Trim to the BASIC BLOCK/D-2/STRIP SET

SEGMENT width of 16-1/2", if necessary. Sew these to the
remaining sides of the BASIC BLOCK. Press seams away
from the BASIC BLOCK.

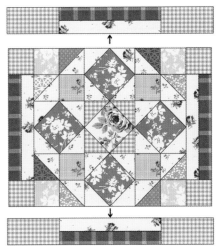

Corner Triangles

Draw a diagonal line across the wrong side of the
4-1/2" WHITE SPRIGS (A-3) squares. With right sides
together, place the 4-1/2" squares on each corner of the
three Block 3. Stitch on the drawn line. Press toward
the outside corner. Trim away excess fabric. BLOCK 3
measures 16-1/2" square.

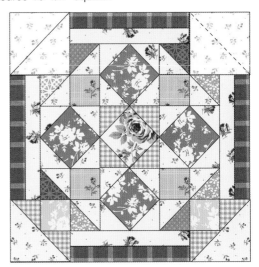

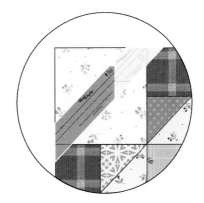

*Note: Piggy
Backing
BerriAngles® is an
option for this step.
See page 11 in the
BerriAngles®
Section.*

Cutting Instructions
Pieced Setting Triangles
Make 12 Triangles

Fabric A WHITE SPRIGS:
    Cut (1) 72" x Full Width of Fabric rectangle.
      Trim off selvage and cut lengthwise:
        (4) 6" x 72" strips   (A-4)
        (4) 3-3/8" x 72" strips   (A-5)

Fabric I BLUE WINDOW PANE:
    Cut (8) 3-3/4" x 40" strips.   (I-5)

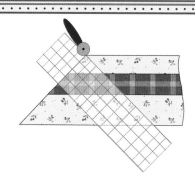

Piecing Setting Triangles
Strip Set

1. Trim the selvages from the 3-3/4" x 40" BLUE WINDOW PANE (I-5) strips. Sew ends together in pairs to make four long strips; press. Trim each strip to 72" in length.

Make 4

2. Sew together the long edges of a 6" x 54" WHITE SPRIGS (A-4), a 3-3/4" x 54" BLUE WINDOW PANE (I-5), and a 3-3/8" x 54" WHITE SPRIGS (A-5) strip; press seams toward dark fabric. The strip set measures 12-3/8" x 54". Make six strip sets.

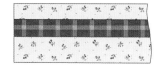

Make 6

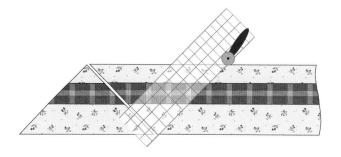

Cut Setting Triangles

Cut twelve triangles from the strip sets made in Step 1 using a ruler or Setting Triangle™ ruler, taking care to cut the triangles with the wide band of WHITE SPRIGS at the bottom.

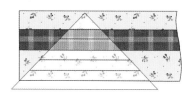

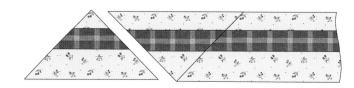

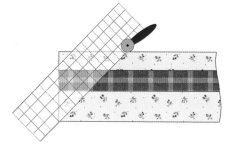

Note: *Save the unused triangles from cutting the pieced setting triangles to make a pillow.*

Quilt Top
Cutting Instructions

Fabric A WHITE SPRIGS:
    Cut (1) 12-1/2" X 40" strip.
      From this strip cut:
      (2) 12-1/2" squares;
      cut each in half diagonally to
      make four Corner Triangles   (A-6)

Piecing the Quilt Top
Assemble Rows

Lay out sixteen Block 1, nine Block 2, twelve Setting Triangles, and four WHITE SPRIGS (A-6) Corner Triangles on a large flat surface as shown. Sew the blocks and Setting Triangles together in diagonal rows. Do not join the Corner Triangles at this time. Press seams toward the Setting Triangles and Block 2.

HINT: *When joining a Setting Triangle to a block, align the fabrics at one edge and let the Setting Triangle extend beyond the opposite edge of the block as shown.*

2. Join the two sections; press all row seams in one direction. Add the WHITE SPRIGS (A-6) Corner Triangles with the longest edge of the triangle next to the block. Press seams toward the triangles. Trim the quilt edges to allow for a 1/4" seam allowance.

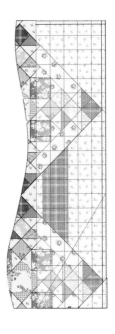

Joining the Rows

1. Match seams and pin for best results. Stitch rows one, two, three, and four together for one section. Then stitch rows five, six, and seven together.

Pillow Tuck Section Cutting Instructions

Fabric A WHITE SPRIGS:
    Cut (2) 16-1/2" x 40" strips
        From these strips cut:
        (2) 6" x 16-1/2" rectangles   (A-7)
        (2) 16" x 16-1/2" rectangles   (A-8)

Fabric I BLUE WINDOW PANE:
    Cut (5) 2" x 40" strips so stripes match   (I-6)

Piecing the Pillow Tuck
Prepare Accent Strips

Trim selvages from the five 2" x 40" BLUE WINDOW PANE (I-6) strips. Sew ends together to make one long strip, matching the stripes; press. Measure the width of the Quilt Top; ours is 90-1/2". Use this measurement to cut two accent strips from the long strip.

Assemble Pillow Tuck

1. Trim the two 6" x 16-1/2" WHITE SPRINGS (A-7) rectangles and the two 16" x 16-1/2" WHITE SPRIGS (A-8) rectangles to the measurement of your 3 blocks, if necessary.

2. Lay out three Block 3, two 6" x 16-1/2" WHITE SPRIGS (A-7) rectangles, two 16" x 16-1/2" WHITE SPRIGS (A-8) rectangles, and two BLUE WINDOW PANE accent strips on a large flat surface as shown. Sew the blocks and rectangles together; press seams away from blocks. Add the accent strips. Press seams toward the strips.

3. Trim the PILLOW TUCK section to the width of the QUILT TOP, if necessary. Sew the Pillow Tuck to the Quilt Top.

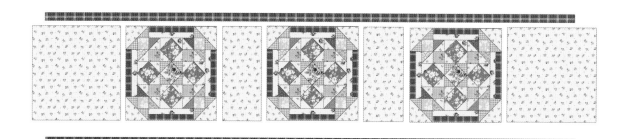

Finishing The Quilt
Cutting Instructions

Backing Fabric BLUE RELIEF FLORAL:
   Cut (3) 96" x Full Width of Fabric rectangles.

Binding Fabric BLUE WINDOW PANE:
   Cut enough 2-1/4" wide bias strips to make a 410" long strip.

Piecing the Backing

Trim the selvages from the edges of the three backing rectangles. Sew the long edges of the rectangles together, using a 1/2" seam allowance. Press the seams open.

Quilting

Layer the pieced backing, batting, and quilt top. Baste the layers together and machine- or hand-quilt as desired. See page 5 in the General Instructions for more information.

Adding the Binding

Prepare the binding and sew to the quilt using a 1/4" seam allowance. Fold the binding to the back to cover the machine stitching and slip-stitch in place.

Lakeside Villa

Villa
Garden

Color Option

Villa Garden

Three pieced blocks and pieced setting triangles make this beautifully intricate quilt a work of art. Golden sunflowers and beautiful green hues create a Villa Garden look for your bedroom. This queen quilt has a pieced pillow tuck for a finished look.

Fabrics & Supplies

Finished Size: 90" x 108" • Block Size: 16"

A—4-1/8 yards ECRU TINY FLORAL
    All Blocks

B—5/8 yard each of FOUR MEDIUM GREEN PRINTS
    All Blocks

C—5/8 yard GREEN FILIGREE
    All Blocks

D—1-7/8 yards DARK GREEN PRINT
    All Blocks

E—2-1/4 yards GOLD FILIGREE
    All Blocks

F—4 yards ECRU LARGE FLORAL
    Blocks 2 and 3, Setting Triangles,
    Corner Triangles and Pillow Tuck

G—2-1/4 yards ECRU/GREEN STRIPE
    All Blocks, Setting Triangles and Accent Strips

Binding—1 yard ECRU/GREEN STRIPE

Backing—8 yards ECRU LARGE FLORAL

Batting—96" x 114" rectangle

Optional—Half- Square BerriAngles®
    176—2" Finished

Optional—Folded Corner BerriAngles®
    560—2" Finished
    48—3" Finished
    48—1" Finished

NOTE: *See Piggy-Back Method in BerriAngles® Section.*

Before beginning this project,
see General Instructions on pages 5-7.

Cutting Instructions

Basic Block
Make 28 Blocks

Note: *If your Fabric A measures at least 42-1/2" wide, you will only need to cut (20) 2-1/2" strips for the 2-1/2" (A-2) squares. If your Fabric D measures at least 40-1/2" wide, you will only need to cut (13) 4-1/2" strips for the 4-1/2" (D-1) squares.*

Fabric A ECRU TINY FLORAL:
    Cut (16) 2-7/8" x 40" strips.   (A-1)
    (21) 2-1/2" x 40" strips.
        From the strips cut:
        (336) 2-1/2" squares   (A-2)

Fabric B FOUR MEDIUM GREEN PRINTS:
    Cut (4) 2-7/8" x 40" strips from each
    print to total 16 strips.   (B-1)
    (2) 2-1/2" x 40" strips from each print to total 8 strips.
        From the strips cut:
        (28) 2-1/2" squares from each print
        to total 112 squares   (B-2)

Fabric C GREEN FILIGREE:
    Cut (7) 2-1/2" x 40" strips.
        From the strips cut:
        (112) 2-1/2" squares   (C-1)

Fabric D DARK GREEN PRINT:
    Cut (14) 4-1/2" x 40" strips.
        From the strips cut:
        (112) 4-1/2" squares   (D-1)

Fabric E GOLD FILIGREE:
    Cut (4) 4-1/2" x 40" strips.
        From the strips cut:
        (28) 4-1/2" squares   (E-1)

Fabric G ECRU/GREEN STRIPE:
    Cut (14) 2-1/2" x 40" strips.
        From the strips cut:
        (224) 2-1/2" squares   (G-1)

Piecing the Basic Block

Half-Square Triangle Units

Make 352

1. With right sides together, layer the 2-7/8" x 40" ECRU TINY FLORAL (A-1) and MEDIUM GREEN PRINTS (B-1) strips in pairs for a total of sixteen strip pairs; press. Cut the layered pairs into 2-7/8" squares, cutting (44) 2-7/8" squares from each of the four ECRU TINY FLORAL/MEDIUM GREEN PRINT fabric combinations.

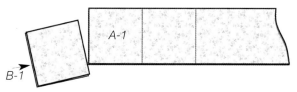

2. Keeping the above squares together in pairs, use a 2" Finished Half-Square BerriAngles® or draw a diagonal line across the wrong side of all the ECRU TINY FLORAL (A-1) squares. Stitch 1/4" on both sides of the drawn line. Cut apart on the drawn line; press seams toward dark triangle. The HALF-SQUARE TRIANGLES measure 2-1/2" square. Make 88 HALF-SQUARE TRIANGLES from each MEDIUM GREEN PRINT for a total of 352 to be used for the BIRD-IN-AIR units and BLOCK 1.

Traditional Method

BerriAngles® Method

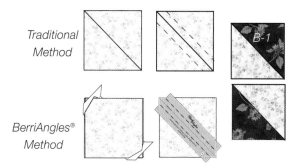

Bird-in-Air Units

Make 112

1. Arrange one 2-1/2" MEDIUM GREEN PRINT (B-2) square, one 2-1/2" GREEN FILIGREE (C-1) square, and two HALF-SQUARE TRIANGLES with different greens (made in Step 1). Sew the squares and half-square triangles together in pairs; press seams toward the squares. Sew the pairs together; press. The BIRD-IN-AIR unit measures 4-1/2" square. Make 112.

Make 112

Square-in-a-Square Units

GOLD CENTER

Make 28

Use 2" Finished Folded Corner BerriAngles® or draw a diagonal line across the wrong side of (112) 2-1/2" ECRU TINY FLORAL (A-2) squares. With right sides together, place 2-1/2" ECRU TINY FLORAL squares on opposite corners of a 4-1/2" GOLD FILIGREE (E-1) square as diagrammed. Stitch on the drawn lines. Press toward the outside corners. Trim away excess fabric if desired. Repeat for the remaining corners. The SQUARE-IN-A-SQUARE unit measures 4-1/2" square. Make 28.

Traditional Method

BerriAngles® Method

Make 28

GREEN CENTER

Make 112

Use 2" Finished Folded Corner BerriAngles® or draw a diagonal line across the wrong side of the remaining (224) 2-1/2" ECRU TINY FLORAL (A-2) squares and all 2-1/2" ECRU/GREEN STRIPE (G-1) squares. With right sides together, place a 2-1/2" ECRU TINY FLORAL square and a 2-1/2" ECRU/GREEN STRIPE square on opposite corners of a 4-1/2" DARK GREEN PRINT (D-1) square as diagrammed. Stitch on the drawn lines. Press toward the outside corners. Trim away excess fabric if desired. Repeat for the remaining corners. The SQUARE-IN-A-SQUARE unit measures 4-1/2" square. Make 112.

Traditional Method

BerriAngles® Method

Make 112

Joining the Units

1. Lay out four BIRD-IN-AIR units, four DARK GREEN CENTER SQUARE-IN-A-SQUARE units, and one GOLD CENTER SQUARE-IN-A-SQUARE unit as shown. Make sure the DARK GREEN CENTER SQUARE-IN-A-SQUARE units are placed with the ECRU/GREEN STRIPE fabric next to the GOLD CENTER SQUARE-IN-A-SQUARE.

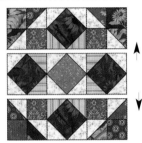

2. Sew the units together in rows. Press the seam allowances away from the DARK GREEN CENTER SQUARE-IN-A-SQUARE units. Sew the rows together; press. The BASIC BLOCK measures 12-1/2" square. Make 28 BASIC BLOCKS.

Note: If your block does not measure 12-1/2" square, you may need to trim some of the units in future steps.

Cutting Instructions

Block 1

Make 16 Blocks

Note: If your Fabric A measures at least 42-1/2" wide, you will only need to cut (13) 2-1/2" strips for the 2-1/2" x 8-1/2" rectangles (A-3).

Fabric A ECRU TINY FLORAL:
Cut (16) 2-1/2" x 40" strips.
From the strips cut:
(64) 2-1/2" x 8-1/2" rectangles   (A-3)

Fabric E GOLD FILIGREE:
Cut (4) 2-1/2" x 40" strips.
From the strips cut:
(64) 2-1/2" squares   (E-2)

Piecing Block 1

1. Position a HALF-SQUARE TRIANGLE (made in Step 1 of Piecing the Basic Block) at each end of a 2-1/2" x 8-1/2" ECRU TINY FLORAL (A-3) rectangle. Place the medium green triangles to mirror each other for the top outside corners of the sewn strips. Sew the HALF-SQUARE TRIANGLES to the rectangles; press seams toward the rectangles. Make 64.

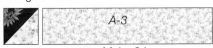

Make 64

2. Position pieced strips from Step 1 on opposite sides of sixteen BASIC BLOCKS so the medium green triangles will again become the outside corners once sewn. Sew the pieced strip in place; press seams away from BASIC BLOCK. Make 16.

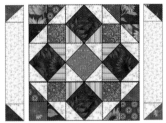

Make 16

3. Sew a 2-1/2" GOLD FILIGREE (E-2) square to each end of the remaining 32 pieced strips from Step 1. Press seams away from the squares. Position these on the two remaining sides of the same 16 BASIC BLOCKS so the medium green triangles will be along the outside edge once sewn. Sew the pieced strip units in place; press seams away from the BASIC BLOCK. The block should measure 16-1/2".

Make 16

Cutting Instructions

Block 2

Make 9 Blocks

Note: If your Fabric F measures at least 40-1/2" wide, you will only need to cut (4) 4-1/2" strips for the 4-1/2" (F-1) squares.

Fabric E GOLD FILIGREE:
Cut (15) 2-1/2" x 40" strips.
From the strips cut:
(18) 2-1/2" x 12-1/2" strips   (E-3)
(18) 2-1/2" x 16-1/2" strips   (E-4)

Fabric F ECRU LARGE FLORAL:
Cut (5) 4-1/2" x 40" strips.
From the strips cut:
(36) 4-1/2" squares   (F-1)

Piecing Block 2

1. Trim the (18) 2-1/2" x 12-1/2" GOLD FILIGREE (E-3) strips to the BASIC BLOCK width, if needed. Sew these to opposite sides of nine BASIC BLOCKS; press toward the strips.

2. Trim the (18) 2-1/2" x 16-1/2" GOLD FILIGREE (E-4) strips to the E-3/BASIC BLOCK width, if needed. Sew these to the remaining sides of the nine BASIC BLOCKS; press toward the strips.

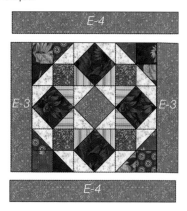

3. Draw a diagonal line across the wrong side of the 4-1/2" ECRU LARGE FLORAL (F-1) squares. With right sides together, place the 4-1/2" squares on each corner of the nine BLOCK 2. Stitch on the drawn line. Press toward the outside corner. Trim away excess fabric. BLOCK 2 measures 16-1/2" square.

Note: Piggy Backing BerriAngles® is an option for this step. See page 11 in the BerriAngle® section.

Cutting Instructions

Block 3

Make 3 Blocks

Fabric A ECRU TINY FLORAL:
Cut (3) 1-1/2" x 40" strips.   (A-4)

Fabric E GOLD FILIGREE:
Cut (3) 1-1/2" x 40" strips.   (E-5)
From the strips cut:
(12) 2-1/2" squares   (E-6)
(12) 2-1/2" x 4-1/2" rectangles   (E-7)

Fabric F ECRU LARGE FLORAL:
Cut (2) 4-1/2" x 40" strips.
From the strips cut:
(12) 4-1/2" squares   (F-2)

Piecing Block 3

1. Sew together the long edges of the 1-1/2" x 40" ECRU TINY FLORAL (A-4) and GOLD FILIGREE (E-5) strips in pairs with right sides together to make strip sets. Press seams toward the dark strips. Cut strip sets into twelve 2-1/2" x 8-1/2" segments.

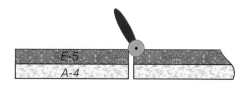

2. Sew a 2-1/2" GOLD FILIGREE (E-6) square to each end of six strip segments from Step 1. Press toward the segments. Trim to the BASIC BLOCK width, if necessary. Sew these to opposite sides of the three remaining BASIC BLOCKS. Press seams away from the BASIC BLOCK.

3. Sew a 2-1/2" x 4-1/2" GOLD FILIGREE (E-7) rectangle to each end of the six remaining strip segments from Step 1; press toward the segments. Trim to the BASIC BLOCK/STRIP SET SEGMENT/E-6 width, if necessary. Sew these to the remaining sides of the BASIC BLOCK. Press seams away from the BASIC BLOCK.

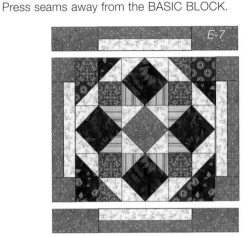

4. Draw a diagonal line across the wrong side of the 4-1/2" ECRU LARGE FLORAL (F-2) squares. With right sides together, place the 4-1/2" squares on each corner of the three Block 3. Stitch on the drawn line. Press toward the outside corner. Trim away excess fabric. BLOCK 3 measures 16-1/2" square.

Note: *Piggy Backing BerriAngles® is an option for this step. See page 11 in the BerriAngles® section.*

Cutting Instructions

Pieced Setting Triangles

Make 12 Triangles

Fabric F ECRU LARGE FLORAL:
Cut (1) 72" x Full Width of Fabric rectangle.
 Trim off selvages and cut lengthwise:
  (4) 6" x 72" strips.   (F-3)
  (4) 3-3/8" x 72" strips. (F-4)

Fabric G ECRU/GREEN STRIPE:
Cut (8) 3-3/4" x 40" strips. (G-2)

Piecing the Setting Triangles

1. Trim selvages from the 3-3/4" x 40" ECRU/GREEN STRIPE (G-2) strips. Sew together in pairs to make four long strips; press. Trim each strip to 72" in length.

2. Sew together the long edges of a 6" x 72" ECRU LARGE FLORAL (F-3) strip, a 3-3/4" x 72" ECRU/GREEN STRIPE (G-2), and a 3-3/8" x 72" ECRU LARGE FLORAL (F-4) strip; press seams toward dark fabric. The strip set measures 12-3/8" x 72". Make four strip sets.

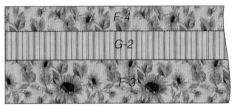

Make 4

3. Cut twelve triangles from the strip sets made in Step 2 using a ruler or a Setting Triangle™ ruler with a 45-degree marking, taking care to cut the triangles with the wide band of ECRU LARGE FLORAL at the bottom.

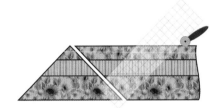

Note: *You will only use the triangle with the wide fabric band at the bottom for the quilt. Save the unused triangles to make a pillow.*

Quilt Top Cutting Instructions

Fabric F ECRU LARGE FLORAL:
Cut (1) 12-1/2" X 40" strip.
 From this strip cut:
  (2) 12-1/2" squares; cut each in half diagonally
  to make 4 Corner Triangles (F-5)

Piecing the Quilt Top

1. Lay out sixteen Block 1, nine Block 2, twelve Setting Triangles, and four ECRU LARGE FLORAL (F-5) Corner Triangles on a large flat surface as shown. Sew the blocks and Setting Triangles together in diagonal rows. Do not join the Corner Triangles at this time. Press seams toward the Setting Triangles and Block 2.

Note: *When joining a Setting Triangle to a block, align the fabrics at one edge and let the Setting Triangle extend beyond the opposite edge of the block.*

2. For best results, match seams and pin when joining rows. Stitch rows one, two, three, and four together for one section. Then stitch rows five, six, and seven together.

3. Join the two sections; press all row seams in one direction. Add the ECRU LARGE FLORAL (F-5) Corner Triangles with the longest edge of the triangle next to the block. Press seams toward the triangles. Trim the quilt edges to allow for a 1/4" seam allowance.

Pillow Tuck Cutting Instructions

Fabric F ECRU LARGE FLORAL:
    Cut (1) 6" x 40" strip.
        From the strip cut:
        (2) 6" x 16-1/2" rectangles   (F-6)
    (1) 16" x 40" strip.
        From the strip cut:
        (2) 16" x 16-1/2" rectangles   (F-7)

Fabric G ECRU/GREEN STRIPE:
    Cut (5) 2" x 40" strips.   (G-3)

Piecing the Pillow Tuck

1. Trim selvages from the five 2" x 40" ECRU/GREEN STRIPE (G-3) strips. Sew ends together to make one long strip; press. Measure the width of the Quilt Top; ours is 90-1/2". Use this measurement to cut two accent strips from the long strip.

2. Trim the two 6" x 16-1/2" ECRU LARGE FLORAL (F-6) rectangles and the two 16" x 16-1/2" ECRU LARGE FLORAL (F-7) rectangles to the measurement of your #3 blocks, if necessary. Lay out three Block 3, two 6" x 16-1/2" ECRU LARGE FLORAL (F-6) rectangles, two 16" x 16-1/2" ECRU LARGE FLORAL (F-7) rectangles, and two ECRU/GREEN STRIPE accent strips (from Step 1) on a large flat surface as shown. Sew the blocks and rectangles together; press seams away from blocks. Center and add the accent strips. Press seams toward strips.

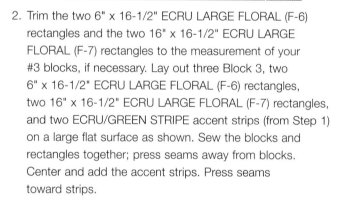

3. Trim the Pillow Tuck to the width of the Quilt Top, if necessary. Sew the Pillow Tuck to the Quilt Top. Press seam toward Pillow Tuck.

Finishing the Quilt Cutting Instructions

Backing Fabric ECRU LARGE FLORAL:
    Cut (3) 96" x Full Width of Fabric rectangles.

Binding Fabric ECRU/GREEN STRIPE:
    Cut enough 2-1/4" wide bias strips to make a 410" long strip.

Finishing the Quilt

1. Trim the selvages from the edges of the three backing rectangles. Sew the long edges of the rectangles together, using a 1/2" seam allowance. Press the seams open.

2. Layer the pieced backing, batting, and quilt top. Baste the layers together and machine- or hand-quilt as desired. See page 5 in the General Instructions for more information.

3. Prepare the binding and sew to the quilt front using a 1/4" seam allowance. Fold the binding to the back to cover the machine stitching and slip-stitch in place. See Bias Binding on page 7 for complete directions.

Villa Garden

Villa Pillows

Euro Sham

Fabrics & Supplies

Finished Size: 33-1/2" x 33-1/2"

A—3/4 yard TINY FLORAL
          BACKGROUND
          Block and
          Setting Triangles

B—1/3 yard GOLD FILIGREE
          Block

C—1/4 yard DARK GREEN TONE-ON-TONE
          Block

D—1/3 yard STRIPE
          Block and Inner Border

E—1/4 yard GREEN FILIGREE
          Block

F—1/4 yard, fat quarter or scraps of
          FOUR MEDIUM GREEN PRINTS
          Block

G—5/8 yard LARGE FLORAL
          Block and Outer Border

Backing—1-1/8 yards TINY FLORAL BACKGROUND

Sham back—2 yards LARGE FLORAL

Binding—3/4 yard STRIPE

Batting—40" x 40" square

Optional—Half-Square BerriAngles®
          4—2" Finished

Optional—Folded Corner BerriAngles®
          20—2" Finished
          4—3" Finished
          4—1" Finished

Before beginning this project,
see General Instructions on pages 5-7.

Cutting Instructions

Villa Euro Sham Front

Fabric A TINY FLORAL BACKGROUND:
  Cut (1) 2-7/8" x 40" strip.
        From the strip cut:
        (4) 2-7/8" squares   (A-1)
  (1) 2-1/2" x 40" strip.
        From the strip cut:
        (12) 2-1/2" squares   (A-2)
  (1) 1-1/2" x 40" strip.   (A-3)
  (1) 12-1/2" x 40" strip.
        From the strip cut:
        (2) 12-1/2" squares; cut each in half diagonally
        to make 4 setting triangles   (A-4)

Fabric B GOLD FILIGREE:
  Cut (1) 4-1/2" square   (B-1)
  (1) 1-1/2" x 40" strip.   (B-2)
  (1) 2-1/2" x 40" strip.
        From the strip cut:
        (4) 2-1/2" squares   (B-3)
        (4) 2-1/2" x 4-1/2" rectangles   (B-4)

Fabric C DARK GREEN TONE-ON-TONE:
  Cut (1) 4-1/2" x 40" strip.
        From the strip cut:
        (4) 4-1/2" squares   (C-1)

Fabric D STRIPE:
  Cut (1) 2-1/2" x 40" strip.
        From the strip cut:
        (8) 2-1/2" squares   (D-1)
  (4) 1-1/2" x 40" strips.
        From the strips cut:
        (2) 1-1/2" x 23-1/2" inner border strips   (D-2)
        (2) 1-1/2" x 25-1/2" inner border strips   (D-3)

Fabric E GREEN FILIGREE:
  Cut (1) 2-1/2" x 40" strip.
        From the strip cut:
        (4) 2-1/2" squares   (E-1)

Fabric F FOUR MEDIUM GREEN PRINTS:
  Cut (1) 2-7/8" square from each print
        for a total of four   (F-1)
  (1) 2-1/2" square from each print
        for a total of four   (F-2)

Fabric G LARGE FLORAL:
  Cut (4) 4-1/2" x 40" strips.
        From the strips cut:
        (2) 4-1/2" x 25-1/2" outer border strips   (G-1)
        (2) 4-1/2" x 33-1/2" outer border strips   (G-2)
        (4) 4-1/2" squares   (G-3)

Piecing the Center Block

1. With right sides together, layer the 2-7/8" TINY FLORAL BACKGROUND (A-1) squares with four MEDIUM GREEN PRINTS (F-1) squares. Use a 2" Finished Half-Square BerriAngle® or draw a diagonal line across the wrong side of all the TINY FLORAL BACKGROUND (A-1) squares. Stitch 1/4" on both sides of the drawn line. Cut apart on the drawn line; press seams toward dark triangle. The HALF-SQUARE TRIANGLES measure 2-1/2" square. Make 8 HALF-SQUARE TRIANGLES.

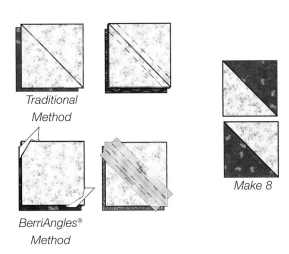

Traditional Method

BerriAngles® Method

Make 8

2. Arrange one 2-1/2" GREEN FILIGREE (E-1) square, one 2-1/2" MEDIUM GREEN PRINT (F-2) square, and two HALF-SQUARE TRIANGLES with different greens (made in Step 1). Sew the squares and half-square triangles together in pairs; press seams toward the squares. Sew the pairs together to complete one BIRD-IN-AIR unit that measures 4-1/2" square; press. Make four.

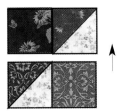

Make 4

3. Use 2" Finished Folded Corner BerriAngles® or draw a diagonal line across the wrong side of four 2-1/2" TINY FLORAL BACKGROUND (A-2) squares. With right sides together, place 2-1/2" TINY FLORAL BACKGROUND squares on opposite corners of the 4-1/2" GOLD FILIGREE (B-1) square as diagrammed. Stitch on the drawn lines. Press toward the outside corners. Trim away

excess fabric if desired. Repeat for the remaining corners. The GOLD CENTER SQUARE-IN-A-SQUARE unit measures 4-1/2" square.

Traditional Method

BerriAngles® Method

Make 1

4. Use 2" Finished Folded Corner BerriAngles® or draw a diagonal line across the wrong side of the remaining eight 2-1/2" TINY FLORAL BACKGROUND (A-2) squares and all 2-1/2" STRIPE (D-1) squares. With right sides together, place a 2-1/2" TINY FLORAL BACKGROUND square and a 2-1/2" STRIPE square on opposite corners of a 4-1/2" DARK GREEN TONE-ON-TONE (C-1) square as diagrammed. Stitch on the drawn lines. Press toward the outside corners. Trim away excess fabric if desired. Repeat for the remaining corners. The GREEN CENTER SQUARE-IN-A-SQUARE unit measures 4-1/2" square. Make four.

5. Lay out four BIRD-IN-AIR units, four GREEN

Traditional Method

BerriAngles® Method

Make 4

CENTER SQUARE-IN-A-SQUARE units, and one GOLD CENTER SQUARE-IN-A-SQUARE unit as shown. Make sure the GREEN CENTER SQUARE-IN-A-SQUARE units are placed with the STRIPE fabric next to the GOLD CENTER SQUARE-IN-A-SQUARE.

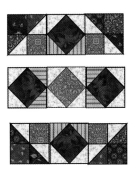

6. Sew the units together in rows. Press the seam allowances away from the GREEN CENTER SQUARE-IN-A-SQUARE units. Sew the rows together; press. The Center Block measures 12-1/2" square.

Adding the Block Border

1. Sew together the long edges of the 1-1/2" x 40" TINY FLORAL BACKGROUND (A-3) and GOLD FILIGREE (B-2) strips with right sides together to make a strip set. Press seams toward the dark strip. Cut strip set into four 2-1/2" x 8-1/2" segments.

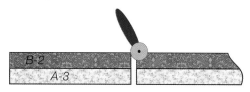

2. Sew a 2-1/2" GOLD FILIGREE (B-3) square to each end of two strip segments from Step 1. Press toward the segments. Trim to the Center Block width, if necessary. Sew these to opposite sides of the Center Block. Press seams away from the Center Block.

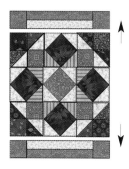

3. Sew a 2-1/2" x 4-1/2" GOLD FILIGREE (B-4) rectangle to each end of the two remaining strip segments from Step 1; press toward the segments. Trim to the Center Block/Strip Segment/B-3 width, if necessary. Sew these to the remaining sides of the Center Block. Press seams away from the Center Block.

4. Draw a diagonal line across the wrong side of the 4-1/2" LARGE FLORAL (G-3) squares. With right sides together, place the 4-1/2" squares on each corner of the Center Block. Stitch on the drawn line. Press toward the outside corner. Trim away excess fabric. Block measures 16-1/2" square.

Note: Piggy Backing BerriAngles® is an option for this step. See page 11 in the BerriAngles® section.

Adding the Sham Borders

1. Stitch TINY FLORAL BACKGROUND (A-4) setting triangles to opposite sides of the completed block. Press seams toward triangles. Sew the two remaining setting triangles (A-4) to the remaining sides of the block to complete the sham center. Press seams toward triangles.

2. Stitch a 1-1/2" x 23-1/2" STRIPE (D-2) inner border strip to opposite sides of the sham center. Press seams toward inner border. Stitch a 1-1/2" x 25-1/2" STRIPE (D-3) inner border strip to the remaining sides of the sham center. Press toward inner border.

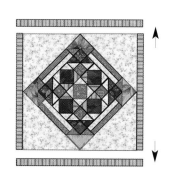

3. Stitch a 4-1/2" x 25-1/2" LARGE FLORAL (G-1) outer border strip to opposite sides of the sham center. Press toward the outer border. Stitch a 4-1/2" x 33-1/2" LARGE FLORAL (G-2) outer border strip to the remaining sides of the sham center. Press toward the outer border.

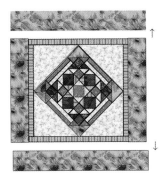

Finishing the Euro Sham
Cutting Instructions

Fabric G LARGE FLORAL:
  Cut (2) 37-1/2" x 33-1/2" rectangles.   (G-4)

Binding STRIPE:
  Cut enough 2-1/2"-wide bias strips to make 170" long strip.

Finishing the Sham

1. Layer the TINY FLORAL BACKGROUND backing fabric, batting, and sham front. Baste the layers together and machine- or hand-quilt as desired. See page 5 in the General Instructions for more information.

2. Trim any excess batting and backing even with the raw edge of the pieced sham front, allowing for a 1/4" seam allowance.

3. Fold each of the 37-1/2" x 33-1/2" LARGE FLORAL (G-4) rectangles in half with wrong sides facing, aligning the 33-1/2" edges opposite the fold; press. The back rectangles measure 18-3/4" x 33-1/2".

4. Smooth the quilted sham front, right side down, on a flat surface. Position a back rectangle on one half of the front, aligning three edges with the fold near the center. Position the second back rectangle over the remaining half of the front in the same manner. The rectangles will overlap approximately 4". Baste the layers together, 1/4" from the raw edges.

5. To create the flange, sew through all layers, stitching-in-the-ditch on the seam that joins the LARGE FLORAL outer border to the STRIPE inner border.

6. Prepare the binding and sew to the sham front using a 1/4" seam allowance. Fold the binding to the back to cover the machine stitching and slip-stitch in place. See Bias Binding on page 7 for complete directions.

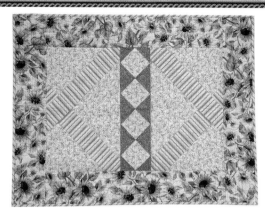

Standard Sham

Fabrics & Supplies

Finished Size: 39-1/2" x 30-1/2"

Note: *Yardage and Cutting Instructions are for two shams. Repeat sewing instructions to make a second sham.*

A—1-1/2 yards TINY FLORAL
  Sham Center

B—1/3 yard GOLD PRINT
  Sham Center

C—1 yard STRIPE
  Sham Center

D—1-1/2 yards LARGE FLORAL
  Border

Backing—2 yards TINY FLORAL

Sham back—5-1/4 yards LARGE FLORAL

Binding—7/8 yard STRIPE

Batting—(2) 44" x 35" rectangles

Optional—Folded Corner BerriAngles®
  32—2" Finished
  32—1-1/2" Finished

Before beginning this project,
see General Instructions on page 5-7.

Cutting Instructions
Villa Sham Front

Fabric A TINY FLORAL:
 Cut (2) 5-1/2" x 40" strips.
  From the strips cut:
  (8) 5-1/2" squares   (A-1)
 (2) 20-1/2" x 40" strips.
  From the strips cut:
  (4) 12-1/2" x 20-1/2" rectangles (A-2)

Fabric B GOLD PRINT:
 Cut (3) 3" x 40" strips.
  From the strips cut:
  (32) 3" squares   (B-1)

Fabric C STRIPE:
 Cut (4) 6-1/2" x 40" strips.
  From the strips cut:
  (8) 6-1/2" x 20" rectangles (C-1)

Fabric D LARGE FLORAL:
 Cut (8) 5-1/2" x 40" strips.
  From the strips cut:
  (4) 5-1/2" x 29-1/2" border strips (D-1)
  (4) 5-1/2" x 30-1/2" border strips (D-2)

Piecing the Sham Front

1. Draw a diagonal line across the wrong side of (16) 3" GOLD PRINT (B-1) squares. With right sides together, place 3" GOLD PRINT squares on opposite corners of a 5-1/2" TINY FLORAL (A-1) square as diagrammed. Stitch on the drawn line. Press toward the outside corners. Trim away excess fabric. Repeat for the remaining corners to complete a SQUARE-IN-A-SQUARE unit that measures 5-1/2" square. Make four.

Traditional Method

BerriAngles® Method

Make 4

Note: *Piggy Backing BerriAngles® Folded Corners is an option for this step. See page 11 in the BerriAngle® Section.*

2. Sew the four SQUARE-IN-A-SQUARE units together to make the center strip. Press seams in one direction.

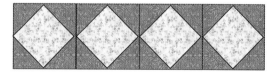

3. With right sides together, fold a 6-1/2" x 20" STRIPE (C-1) rectangle in half to align the long edges. Sew the long edges together, forming a tube. Turn the tube right side out. Press, centering the seam on the back. Make four.

Make 4

4. Mark the center of one long edge of two 12-1/2" x 20-1/2" TINY FLORAL (A-2) rectangles. Position two STRIPE tubes from Step 3 on each TINY FLORAL rectangle so the tubes

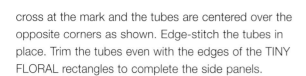

cross at the mark and the tubes are centered over the opposite corners as shown. Edge-stitch the tubes in place. Trim the tubes even with the edges of the TINY FLORAL rectangles to complete the side panels.

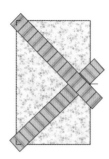

5. Sew a side panel to each long edge of the center strip for the sham center; press seams toward the side panels.

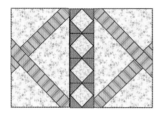

6. Sew a 5-1/2" x 29-1/2" LARGE FLORAL (D-1) border strip to the top and bottom edges of the sham center. Press seams toward the strips. Sew a 5-1/2" x 30-1/2" RELIEF FLORAL (D-2) border strip to the remaining edges of the sham center. Press seams toward the strips.

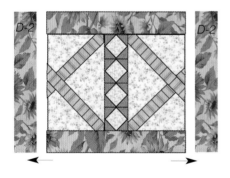

Finishing the Sham Cutting Instructions

Backing TINY FLORAL:
    Cut (2) 44" x 35" backing rectangles.

Sham Back LARGE FLORAL:
    Cut (4) 43-1/2" x 30-1/2" rectangles.

Binding STRIPE:
    Cut enough 2-1/2"-wide bias strips
    to make a 290" long strip.

Finishing the Sham

1. Smooth a TINY FLORAL backing rectangle, right side down, on a flat surface. Center the batting on the backing rectangle and the pieced sham front, right side up, on the batting. Baste the layers together and machine- or hand-quilt as desired.

2. Trim any excess batting and backing even with the raw edge of the pieced sham front, allowing for a 1/4" seam allowance.

3. Fold two of the 43-1/2" x 30-1/2" LARGE FLORAL rectangles in half with wrong sides facing, aligning the 30-1/2" edges opposite the fold; press. The back rectangles measure 21-3/4" x 30-1/2".

4. Smooth the quilted sham front, right side down, on a flat surface. Position a back rectangle on one half of the front, aligning three edges with the fold near the center. Position the second back rectangle over the remaining half of the front in the same manner. The rectangles will overlap approximately 4". Baste the layers together 1/4" from the raw edges.

5. To create the flange, sew through all layers, stitching-in-the-ditch on the seam that joins the LARGE FLORAL border to the sham center.

6. Prepare the binding and sew to the sham front using a 1/4" seam allowance. Fold the binding to the back to cover the machine stitching and slip-stitch in place. See Bias Binding on page 7 for complete directions.

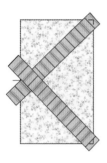

Round Accent Pillow

Fabrics & Supplies

Finished Size: 16" diameter

A—1/3 yard ECRU LARGE FLORAL
Front and Back

B—1/3 yard SMALL GREEN FLORAL
Front and Back

C—Fat Quarter of ECRU/GREEN STRIPE
Front and Back

D—Fat Quarter of GOLD FILIGREE
Front and Back

Backing—5/8 yard ECRU LARGE FLORAL

Binding—1/2 yard ECRU/GREEN STRIPE

Batting—(2) 20" squares and scrap

Optional—Half-Square BerriAngles®
8—4" Finished

Template plastic

Water-soluble marking pen

16" round pillow form

(2) 1-1/8" metal buttons to cover

Quilting thread

Large needle

Before beginning this project,
see General Instructions on pages 5-7.

Cutting Instructions

Pillow Cover

Fabric A ECRU LARGE FLORAL:	
Cut (1) 4-7/8" x 40" strip.	(A-1)
(1) 4-1/2" x 40" strip.	
From the strip cut:	
(8) 4-1/2" squares	(A-2)
Fabric B GREEN SMALL FLORAL:	
Cut (1) 4-7/8" x 40" strip.	(B-1)
(1) 4-1/2" x 40" strip.	
From the strip cut:	
(8) 4-1/2" squares	(B-2)
Fabric C ECRU/GREEN STRIPE:	
Cut (1) 4-7/8" x 20" strip.	(C-1)
Fabric D GOLD FILIGREE:	
Cut (1) 4-7/8" x 20" strip.	(D-1)

Piecing the Pillow Cover

1. With right sides together, layer the 4-7/8" ECRU LARGE FLORAL (A-1) and GREEN SMALL FLORAL (B-1) strips; press. Cut the layered strips into (4) 4-7/8" squares.

2. Keeping the above squares together in pairs, use a 4" Finished Half-Square BerriAngles® or draw a diagonal line across the wrong side of all the ECRU LARGE FLORAL (A-1) squares. Stitch 1/4" on both sides of the drawn line. Cut apart on the drawn line; press seams toward dark triangle. The HALF-SQUARE TRIANGLES measure 4-1/2" square. Make eight HALF-SQUARE TRIANGLES.

Traditional Method

BerriAngles® Method

Make 8

3. Repeat Steps 1 and 2 with the 4-7/8" x 20" ECRU/GREEN STRIPE (C-1) and GOLD FILIGREE (D-1) strips to make eight HALF-SQUARE TRIANGLES, making four HALF-SQUARE TRIANGLES with the stripes running vertically and four with the stripes running horizontally.

Make 4   *Make 4*

4. Arrange one 4-1/2" ECRU LARGE FLORAL (A-2), one 4-1/2" GREEN SMALL FLORAL (B-2) square, one HALF-SQUARE TRIANGLE from Step 2, and one HALF-SQUARE TRIANGLE from Step 3. Sew the squares and half-square triangles together in pairs; press seams toward the squares. Sew the pairs together; press. The BIRD-IN-AIR block measures 8-1/2" square. Make eight blocks, four with vertical stripes and four with horizontal stripes as shown.

Make 4   *Make 4*

90

5. Arrange four BIRD-IN-AIR blocks for the front pillow cover. Sew the blocks together in pairs; press the seams in opposite directions. Sew the pairs together; press. Repeat with the remaining blocks for the back pillow cover.

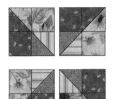

Finishing the Pillow
Cutting Instructions

Backing Fabric—ECRU LARGE FLORAL:
Cut (1) 20" x 40" strip.
From the strip cut:
(2) 20" backing squares

Binding Fabric—ECRU/GREEN STRIPE:
Cut enough 2-3/8"-wide bias strips
to make a 70" long strip.

1. Layer an ECRU LARGE FLORAL backing square, batting, and one pieced pillow cover. Baste the layers together and hand- or machine-quilt as desired. See page 5 in the General Instructions for more information. Repeat for the second pillow cover.

2. Trace the CIRCLE TEMPLATE on page 92 onto template plastic, cut out the shape. Position the template on the upper left BIRD-IN-AIR block of one of the quilted pillow covers. Use a water-soluble marking pen to draw along the curved edge of the template onto the quilted fabric. Reposition the template on each block to complete the drawing. Cut on drawn line. Repeat for the second quilted pillow cover.

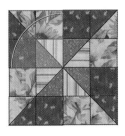

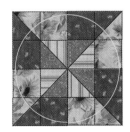

3. With wrong sides together, layer the pillow covers. Prepare the binding and pin it to one side of the layered covers, leaving an 8" gap between the first and last pins and also 8" tails at each end of the binding. Sew binding to the pinned area of the cover with a 1/4" seam allowance,

removing the pins as you sew and leaving an 8" opening between the pins. See Bias Binding on page 7 for complete directions.

4. Insert the pillow form in the opening. Sew the opening closed with a 1/8" seam. Sew to complete the binding with a 1/4" seam, referring to pages 6-7.

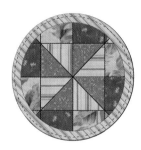

5. To cover the button, place the 1-1/8" metal button on the wrong side of a 3"-square scrap of GREEN SMALL FLORAL. Draw a circle about 1/2" beyond the edge of the button. Place button on a batting scrap, draw around the button exactly at the button's edge. Cut out the fabric and batting circles on the lines. Center the batting circle on the wrong side of the fabric circle, then center the button on the batting. Refer to the package directions to complete the covered button. Make two covered buttons.

6. Thread needle with a 72" length of quilting thread; bring the ends together to double the thread. Working from the center front of the pillow, insert the needle through all layers to the center back of the pillow, leaving a 16" tail at the front. Thread the needle through a button shank at the pillow back and return the needle to the center front of the pillow in the same manner. Thread the needle through the shank of the second button at the pillow front. Return the needle to the back of the pillow; go through the button shank a second time. Return the needle to the pillow front. Cut the thread near the needle, creating another long tail. Loop the thread tails and pull tight to bring the front and back of the pillow together, creating an indentation around the buttons. Knot the thread several times under the button; cut excess thread.

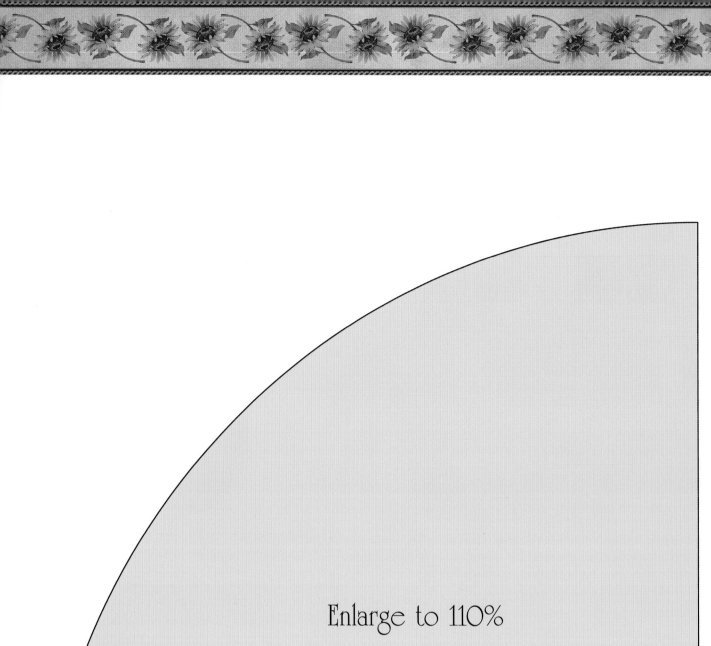

Enlarge to 110%

Pillow Color Option

Villa Square Cloth

Decorate a bedside table with this lovely Villa Square Cloth. It is designed to coordinate with the Villa Garden bedroom ensemble. Because of its size, the square cloth would easily work as a tablecloth for a card table or small table.

Fabrics & Supplies

Finished Size: 50" x 50"

A—2-1/2 yards ECRU LARGE FLORAL
    Front

B—3/4 yard ECRU/GREEN STRIPE
    Front

C—1/2 yard GOLD FILIGREE
    Front

Backing—3-1/4 yards ECRU LARGE FLORAL

Binding—5/8 yard ECRU/GREEN STRIPE

Batting—56" square

Before beginning this project,
see General Instructions on pages 5-7.

Cutting Instructions

Cloth Top

Fabric A ECRU LARGE FLORAL:
Cut (1) 28-1/2" center square.   (A-1)
(1) 52" x Full Width of Fabric rectangle.
    From the rectangle cut:
    (4) 5-1/2" x 52" lengthwise
    border strips   (A-2)

Fabric B ECRU/GREEN STRIPE:
Cut (4) 5-1/2" x 40" strips.
    From the strips cut:
    (2) 5-1/2" x 28-1/2" strips   (B-1)
    (2) 5-1/2" x 38-1/2" strips   (B-2)

Fabric C GOLD FILIGREE:
Cut (1) 16" x 40" strip.
    From the strip cut:
    (2) 16" squares; cut each in half
    diagonally to make four triangles   (C-1)

Piecing the Cloth Top

1. Sew 5-1/2" x 28-1/2" ECRU/GREEN STRIPE (B-1) strips to opposite sides of the 28-1/2" ECRU LARGE FLORAL (A-1) center square. Press seams toward stripes. Sew 5-1/2" x 38-1/2" ECRU/GREEN STRIPE (B-2) strips to the remaining sides of the center square. Press seams toward stripes. The cloth now measures 38-1/2".

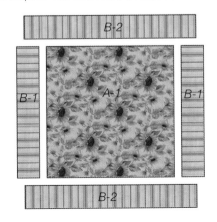

2. Center and sew a GOLD FILIGREE (C-1) triangle to each edge of the cloth. Press seams toward the triangles.

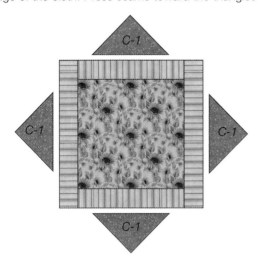

3. Trim all edges of the cloth, allowing for a 1/4" seam allowance beyond the corners of the ECRU LARGE FLORAL (A-1) center square as shown.

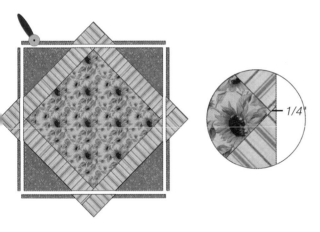

4. Measuring at the center of the pieced cloth, find the length from top to bottom. Use this measurement to trim two 5-1/2" x 52" ECRU LARGE FLORAL (A-2) border strips. Sew these to opposite sides of the pieced cloth. Press seams toward the border.

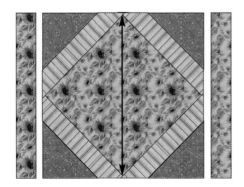

5. Measure the width from side to side at the center of the pieced cloth, including the border strips. Use this

measurement to trim the two remaining 5-1/2" x 52" ECRU LARGE FLORAL (A-2) border strips. Sew these to the remaining sides of the pieced cloth. Press seams toward the border.

Finishing the Cloth Top
Cutting Instructions

Backing Fabric ECRU LARGE FLORAL:
    Cut (2) 58-1/2" x Full Width of Fabric rectangles.

Binding Fabric ECRU/GREEN STRIPE:
    Cut enough 2-1/4"-wide bias strips
    to make a 220" long strip.

Finishing the Cloth

1. Trim the selvages from the edges of the backing rectangles. Sew the long edges of the rectangles together, using a 1/2" seam allowance. Press the seam open.

2. Layer the pieced backing, batting, and cloth top. Baste the layers together and machine- or hand-quilt as desired. See page 5 in the General Instructions for more information.

3. Prepare the binding and sew to the cloth front using a 1/4" seam allowance. Fold the binding to the back to cover the machine stitching and slip-stitch in place. See Bias Binding on page 7 for complete directions.

Sunset Table Runner

Imagine a beautiful garden trellis at sunset. The last flash of color before the sun sets for the day, illuminating the flowers climbing a garden trellis in rich red and gold hues inspired this stunning table runner.

Fabrics & Supplies

Finished Size: 22" x 67"

A—1/2 yard of ECRU TINY FLORAL
    Blocks

B—One Fat Quarter each of FOUR MEDIUM RED PRINTS
    Blocks

C—Fat Quarter RED SHADOWPLAY PRINT
    Blocks

D—Fat Quarter RED TONE-ON-TONE
    Blocks

E—5/8 yard LIGHT GOLD FILIGREE
    Blocks

F—3-1/8 yards RED SMALL FLORAL
    Block Backing, Table Runner Base, and Backing

G—Fat Quarter ECRU/RED STRIPE
    Blocks

H—3/8 yard MEDIUM RED FLORAL
    Blocks

Batting—(3) 20" squares and (1) 20" x 70" rectangle

Binding—1 yard LARGE RED FLORAL

Optional—Half-Square BerriAngles®
    12—2" Finished

Optional—Folded Corner BerriAngles®
    60—2" Finished
    12—3" Finished
    12—1" Finished

Note: *See Piggy-Back Method in BerriAngles®*
    section on page 11.

Before beginning this project,
see the General Instructions on pages 5-7.

Cutting Instructions

Garden Trellis Block

Make Three Blocks

Fabric A ECRU TINY FLORAL:
    Cut (2) 2-7/8" x 40" strips.
        From the strips cut:
        (4) 2-7/8" x 20" strips   (A-1)
    (3) 2-1/2" x 40" strips.
        From the strips cut:
        (36) 2-1/2" squares   (A-2)

Fabric B FOUR MEDIUM RED PRINTS:
    Cut (1) 2-7/8" x 20" strip
        from each print to total 4 strips.   (B-1)
    (1) 2-1/2" x 20" strip for each print to total 4 strips.
        From each strip cut:
        (3) 2-1/2" squares to total 12 squares (B-2)

Fabric C RED SHADOWPLAY PRINT:
    Cut (2) 2-1/2" x 20" strips.
        From the strips cut:
        (12) 2-1/2" squares   (C-1)

Fabric D RED TONE-ON-TONE:
    Cut (3) 4-1/2" x 20" strips.
        From the strips cut:
        (12) 4-1/2" squares   (D-1)

Fabric E LIGHT GOLD FILIGREE:
    Cut (1) 4-1/2" x 40" strip.
        From the strip cut:
        (3) 4-1/2" squares   (E-1)
    (5) 2-1/2" x 40" strips.
        From the strips cut:
        (6) 2-1/2" x 12-1/2" strips   (E-2)
        (6) 2-1/2" x 16-1/2" strips   (E-3)

Fabric G ECRU/RED STRIPE:
    Cut (3) 2-1/2" x 20" strips.
        From the strips cut:
        (24) 2-1/2" squares   (G-1)

Fabric H MEDIUM RED FLORAL:
    Cut (2) 4-1/2" x 40" strips.
        From the strips cut:
        (12) 4-1/2" squares   (H-1)

Piecing the Garden Trellis Block

1. With right sides together, layer the 2-7/8" x 20" ECRU TINY FLORAL (A-1) and the MEDIUM RED PRINTS (B-1) strips in pairs for a total of four strip pairs; press. Cut the layered pairs into 2-7/8" squares, cutting (3) 2-7/8" squares from each of the four fabric combinations for a total of 12 pairs of squares.

2. Keeping the above squares together in pairs, use a 2" Finished Half-Square BerriAngles® or draw a diagonal line across the wrong side of all the ECRU TINY FLORAL (A-1) squares. Stitch 1/4" on both sides of the drawn line. Cut apart on the drawn line; press seams toward the dark triangle. The HALF-SQUARE TRIANGLES measure 2-1/2" square. Make six HALF-SQUARE TRIANGLES from each RED PRINT for a total of 24.

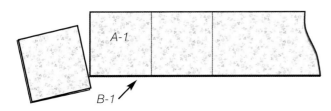

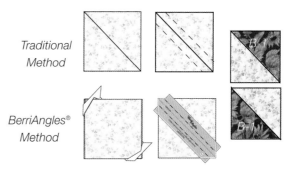

Traditional Method

BerriAngles® Method

3. Arrange one 2-1/2" MEDIUM RED PRINT (B-2) square, one 2-1/2" RED SHADOWPLAY PRINT (C-1) square, and two HALF-SQUARE TRIANGLES with different reds (made in Step 2). Sew the squares and half-square triangles together in pairs; press seams toward the squares. Sew the pairs together to complete one BIRD-IN-AIR unit measuring 4-1/2"; press. Make 12.

Make 12

4. Use 2" Finished Folded Corner BerriAngles® or draw a diagonal line across the wrong side of (12) 2-1/2" ECRU TINY FLORAL (A-2) squares. With right sides together, place 2-1/2" ECRU TINY FLORAL squares on opposite corners of a 4-1/2" LIGHT GOLD FILIGREE (E-1) square as diagrammed. Stitch on the drawn lines. Press toward the outside corners. Trim away excess fabric if desired. Repeat for the remaining corners to complete one GOLD CENTER SQUARE-IN-A-SQUARE unit measuring 4-1/2". Make three.

Traditional Method

BerriAngles® Method *Make 3*

5. Use 2" Finished Folded Corner BerriAngles® or draw a diagonal line across the wrong side of the remaining (24) 2-1/2" ECRU TINY FLORAL (A-2) squares and all ECRU/RED STRIPE (G-1) squares. With right sides together, place a 2-1/2" ECRU TINY FLORAL square and a 2-1/2" ECRU/RED STRIPE square on opposite corners of a 4-1/2" RED TONE-ON-TONE (D-1) square as diagrammed. Stitch on the drawn lines. Press toward the outside corners. Trim away excess fabric if desired. Repeat for the remaining corners to complete one RED CENTER SQUARE-IN-A-SQUARE unit measuring 4-1/2". Make 12.

Traditional Method

BerriAngles® Method *Make 12*

6. Layout four BIRD-IN-AIR units, four RED CENTER SQUARE-IN-A-SQUARE units, and one GOLD CENTER SQUARE-IN-A-SQUARE unit as shown. Make sure the RED CENTER SQUARE-IN-A-SQUARE units are placed with the stripe fabric next to the center SQUARE-IN-A-SQUARE unit. Sew the units together in rows. Press the seam allowances away from the RED CENTER SQUARE-IN-A-SQUARE units. Sew the rows together to complete one BLOCK CENTER measuring 12-1/2"; press. Make three.

Make 3

7. Trim the (6) 2-1/2" x 12-1/2" LIGHT GOLD FILIGREE (E-2) strips to the width of the BLOCK CENTER (made in Step 6), if needed. Sew these to opposite sides of three BLOCK CENTERS; press toward the strips. Trim the (6) 2-1/2" x 16-1/2" LIGHT GOLD FILIGREE (E-3) strips to the E-2/BLOCK CENTER width, if needed. Sew these to the remaining sides of the three BLOCK CENTERS; press toward the strips.

8. Draw a diagonal line across the wrong side of the 4-1/2" MEDIUM RED FLORAL (H-1) squares. With right sides together, place the 4-1/2" squares on each corner of the three blocks from Step 7. Stitch on the drawn lines. Press toward the outside corner. Trim away excess fabric. Garden Trellis block measures 16-1/2" square.

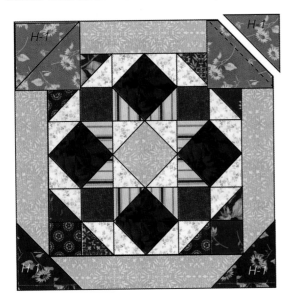

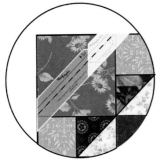

Note: *Piggy Backing BerriAngles® is an option for this step. See page 11 in the BerriAngles® section.*

Finishing The Table Runner
Cutting Instructions

Fabric F RED SMALL FLORAL:
  Cut (2) 20" x 40" strips.
    From the strips cut:
    (3) 20" block backing squares   (F-1)
  (1) 70" x 40" strip.
    From the strip cut:
    (2) 70" x 20" table runner
    base rectangles   (F-2)

Binding LARGE RED FLORAL:
  Cut enough 2-1/4"-wide bias strips
  to make a 430" strip.

1. Layer each pieced block with a 20" batting square and a 20" RED SMALL FLORAL (F-1) backing square. Layer the two 70" x 20" RED SMALL FLORAL (F-2) table runner base rectangles with the 20" x 70" batting rectangle. Baste each set of layers together and machine- or hand-quilt as desired. See page 5 in the General Instructions for more information.

2. Trim each quilted block to 16" square. Prepare binding using the 2-1/4"-wide LARGE RED FLORAL (H-2) bias strips and sew to the front of each quilted block; set aside extra binding for later. Fold the binding to the back to cover the machine stitching and slip-stitch in place. See Bias Binding on page 7 for complete directions.

3. Lay the three blocks on point in a row and measure the width and length as shown. Use these measurements to trim the quilted table runner base.

4. Sew set aside LARGE RED FLORAL binding to the front of the quilted table runner base. Fold the binding to the back to cover the machine stitching and slip-stitch in place. See Bias Binding on page 7 for complete directions.

5. Pin the blocks on the table runner base as shown. Stitch-in-the-ditch along binding seam with matching thread through all layers, securing each block in place.

Color Option

Villa Sunset Quilt

Fabrics & Supplies

Finished Size: 68" x 68"

A—2-1/4 yards BACKGROUND PRINT
    All Blocks

B—1/3 yard each of FOUR RED PRINTS
    All Blocks

C—1/2 yard PINK TONE-ON-TONE
    All Blocks

D—3/4 yard STRIPE
    All Blocks and Setting Triangles

E—1 yard RED TONE-ON-TONE
    All Bocks

F—1-1/8 yards GOLD FILIGREE
    All Blocks

G—1-3/4 yards RED MEDIUM FLORAL
    Block 2 and Setting Triangles

Backing—4-1/8 yards RED MEDIUM FLORAL

Binding—3/4 yard RED MEDIUM FLORAL

Batting—74" square

Optional—Folded Corner BerriAngles®
    260—2" Finished
    16—1" Finished
    16—3" Finished

Optional—Half-Square BerriAngles®
    88—2" Finished

Setting Triangle™ ruler

Before beginning this project,
see General Instructions on page 5-7.

Cutting Instructions

Basic Block

Make 13 Blocks

Note: *If your Fabric E measures at least 42" wide, you will only need to cut (6) 4-1/2"-wide strips for the 4-1/2" (E-1) squares.*

Fabric A BACKGROUND PRINT:
    Cut (8) 2-7/8" x 40" strips.   (A-1)
    (10) 2-1/2" x 40" strips.
        From the strips cut:
        (156) 2-1/2" squares   (A-2)

Fabric B FOUR RED PRINTS:
    Cut (2) 2-7/8" x 40" strips from
    each print to total 8 strips.   (B-1)
    (1) 2-1/2" x 40" strips from each print to total 4 strips.
        From each strip cut:
        (13) 2-1/2" squares to
        total 52 squares   (B-2)

Fabric C PINK TONE-ON-TONE:
    Cut (4) 2-1/2" x 40" strips.
        From the strips cut:
        (52) 2-1/2" squares   (C-1)

Fabric D STRIPE:
    Cut (7) 2-1/2" x 40" strips.
        From the strips cut:
        (104) 2-1/2" squares   (D-1)

Fabric E RED TONE-ON-TONE:
    Cut (7) 4-1/2" x 40" strips.
        From the strips cut:
        (52) 4-1/2" squares   (E-1)

Fabric F GOLD FILIGREE:
    Cut (2) 4-1/2" x 40" strips.
        From the strips cut:
        (13) 4-1/2" squares   (F-1)

Piecing the Basic Block

Half-Square Triangles

Make 176

1. With right sides together, layer the 2-7/8" x 40" BACKGROUND PRINT (A-1) and RED PRINTS (B-1) strips in pairs for a total of eight strip pairs; press. Cut the layered pairs into 2-7/8" squares, cutting (22) 2-7/8" squares from each of the four BACKGROUND PRINT/RED PRINT fabric combinations.

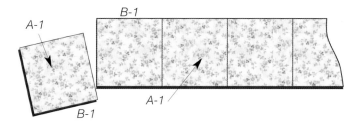

2. Keeping the above squares together in pairs, use a 2" Finished Half-Square BerriAngles® or draw a diagonal line across the wrong side of all the BACKGROUND PRINT (A-1) squares. Stitch 1/4" on both sides of the drawn line. Cut apart on the drawn line; press seams toward dark triangle. The HALF-SQUARE TRIANGLES measure 2-1/2" square. Make 44 HALF-SQUARE TRIANGLES from each RED PRINT for a total of 176 to be used for the BIRD-IN-AIR Units and Block 1.

Traditional Method

BerriAngles® Method

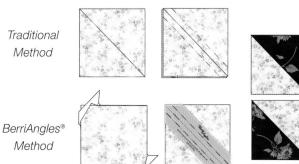

Make 176

Bird-in-Air Units

Make 52

Arrange one 2-1/2" RED PRINT (B-2) square, one 2-1/2" PINK TONE-ON-TONE (C-1) square, and two HALF-SQUARE TRIANGLES with different reds (made in Step 1). Sew the squares and half-square triangles together in pairs; press seams toward the squares. Sew the pairs together; press. The BIRD-IN-AIR unit measures 4-1/2" square. Make 52.

Make 52

Square-in-a-Square Units

Gold Center

Make 13

Use 2" Finished Folded Corner BerriAngles® or draw a diagonal line across the wrong side of (52) 2-1/2" BACKGROUND PRINT (A-2) squares. With right sides together, place 2-1/2" BACKGROUND PRINT squares on opposite corners of a 4-1/2" GOLD FILIGREE (F-1) square as diagrammed. Stitch on the drawn lines. Press toward the outside corners. Trim away excess fabric if desired. Repeat for the remaining corners. The SQUARE-IN-A-SQUARE unit measures 4-1/2" square. Make 13.

Traditional Method

BerriAngles® Method

Make 13

Red Center

Make 52

Use 2" Finished Folded Corner BerriAngles® or draw a diagonal line across the wrong side of (104) 2-1/2" BACKGROUND PRINT (A-2) squares and (104) 2-1/2" STRIPE (D-1) squares. With right sides together, place a 2-1/2" BACKGROUND PRINT square and a 2-1/2" STRIPE square on opposite corners of a 4-1/2" RED TONE-ON-TONE (E-1) square as diagrammed. Stitch on the drawn lines. Press toward the outside corners. Trim away excess fabric if desired. Repeat for the remaining corners. The SQUARE-IN-A-SQUARE unit measures 4-1/2" square. Make 52.

Traditional Method

BerriAngles® Method

Make 52

Joining the Units

1. Lay out four BIRD-IN-AIR units, four RED CENTER SQUARE-IN-A-SQUARE units, and one GOLD CENTER SQUARE-IN-A-SQUARE unit as shown. Make sure the RED CENTER SQUARE-IN-A-SQUARE units are placed with the STRIPE fabric next to the BACKGROUND PRINT fabric of the CENTER SQUARE-IN-A-SQUARE.

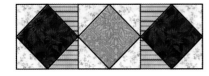

2. Sew the units together in rows. Press the seam allowances away from the RED CENTER SQUARE-IN-A-SQUARE units. Sew the rows together; press. The BASIC BLOCK measures 12-1/2" square. Make 13.

Note: *If your block does not measure 12-1/2" square you may need to trim some of the units in future steps.*

Cutting Instructions

Block 1

Make 9 Blocks

Fabric A BACKGROUND PRINT:
    Cut (9) 2-1/2" x 40" strips.
        From the strips cut:
            (36) 2-1/2" x 8-1/2" rectangles   (A-3)

Fabric F GOLD FILIGREE:
    Cut (3) 2-1/2" x 40" strips.
        From the strips cut:
            (36) 2-1/2" squares   (F-2)

Piecing Block 1

1. Position a HALF-SQUARE TRIANGLE (made in Step 1 of Piecing the Basic Block) at each end of a 2-1/2" x 8-1/2" BACKGROUND PRINT (A-3) rectangle. Place the red triangles to mirror each other for the top outside corners of the sewn strips. Sew the HALF-SQUARE TRIANGLES

to the rectangles; press seams toward the rectangles. Make 36.

Make 36

2. Position pieced strips from Step 1 on opposite sides of nine BASIC BLOCKS so the red triangles will again become the outside corners once sewn. Sew the pieced strips in place; press seams away from the BASIC BLOCK. Make nine.

3. Sew a 2-1/2" GOLD FILIGREE (F-2) square to each end of the remaining 18 pieced strips from Step 1. Press seams away from the squares. Position these on the two remaining sides of the same nine BASIC BLOCKS so the red triangles will be along the outside edge once sewn. Sew the pieced strips in place; press seams away from the BASIC BLOCK.

Make 9

Cutting Instructions

Block 2

Make 4 Blocks

Fabric F GOLD FILIGREE:
    Cut (7) 2-1/2" x 40" strips.
        From the strips cut:
           (8) 2-1/2" x 12-1/2" strips   (F-3)
           (8) 2-1/2" x 16-1/2" strips   (F-4)

Fabric G RED MEDIUM FLORAL:
    Cut (2) 4-1/2" x 40" strips.
    From the strips cut:
    (16) 4-1/2" squares   (G-1)

Piecing Block 2

1. Trim the eight 2-1/2" x 12-1/2" GOLD FILIGREE (F-3) strips to the BASIC BLOCK width, if needed. Sew these to opposite sides of four BASIC BLOCKS; press toward the strips.

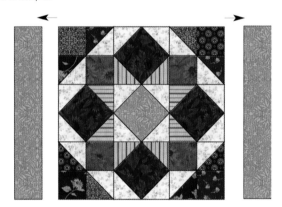

2. Trim the eight 2-1/2" x 16-1/2" GOLD FILIGREE (F-4) strips to the F-3/BASIC BLOCK width, if needed. Sew these to the remaining sides of the four BASIC BLOCKS; press toward the strips.

3. Draw a diagonal line across the wrong side of the 4-1/2" RED MEDIUM FLORAL (G-1) squares. With right sides together, place the 4-1/2" squares on each corner of the four block 2. Stitch on the drawn line. Press toward the outside corner. Trim away excess fabric. Block 2 measures 16-1/2" square.

Note: *Piggy Backing BerriAngles® is an option for this step. See page 11 in the BerriAngles® section.*

Cutting Instructions

Pieced Setting Triangles

Make 12 Triangles

Fabric D STRIPE:
    Cut (4) 3-3/4" x 40" strips.   (D-2)

Fabric G RED MEDIUM FLORAL:
    Cut (4) 6" x 40" strips.   (G-2)
    (4) 3-3/8" x 40" strips.   (G-3)

Piecing the Setting Triangles

1. Sew together the long edges of a 3-38" x 40" RED MEDIUM FLORAL (G-3), a 3-3/4" x 40" STRIPE (D-2), and a 6" x 40" RED MEDIUM FLORAL (G-2) strip as shown; press seams toward dark fabric. The strip set measures 12-3/8" x 40". Make four strip sets.

Make 4

2. Cut eight setting triangles from the strip sets made in Step 1 using a ruler or Setting Triangle™ ruler with a 45-degree marking, taking care to cut the triangles with the wide band of RED MEDIUM FLORAL at the bottom.

Note: *You will only use the triangles with the wide fabric band at the bottom for the quilt. Save the unused triangles to make a pillow.*

Quilt Top Cutting Instructions

Fabric G RED MEDIUM FLORAL:
    Cut (1) 12-1/2" x 40" strip.
        From the strip cut:
        (2) 12-1/2" squares; cut in half
        diagonally to make 4 corner triangles   (G-4)

1. Lay out nine Block 1, four Block 2, eight setting triangles, and four RED MEDIUM FLORAL (G-4) corner triangles on a large flat surface as shown.

Sew the blocks and setting triangles together in diagonal rows. Do not join the corner triangles at this time. Press seams toward the setting triangles and Block 2.

Note: *When joining a setting triangle to a block, align the fabrics at one edge and let the triangle extend beyond the opposite edge of the block.*

2. Sew the rows together, matching seams and pinning for best results. Press all row seams in one direction. Add the RED MEDIUM FLORAL (G-4) corner triangles with the longest edge of the triangle next to the block. Press seams toward the triangles. Trim the quilt edges to allow for a 1/4" seam allowance.

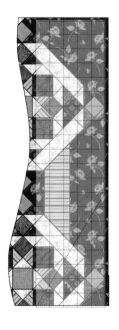

Finishing the Quilt
Cutting Instructions

Backing Fabric - RED MEDIUM FLORAL:
Cut (2) 74" x Full Width of Fabric rectangles

Binding Fabric - RED MEDIUM FLORAL:
Cut enough 2-1/4"-wide bias strips to make a 310" long strip.

Finishing the Quilt

1. Trim the selvages from the edges of the backing rectangles. Sew the long edges of the rectangles together, using a 1/2" seam allowance. Press the seams open.

2. Layer the pieced backing, batting, and quilt top. Baste the layers together and machine- or hand-quilt as desired. See page 5 in the General Instructions for more information.

3. Prepare the binding and sew to the quilt front using a 1/4" seam allowance. Fold the binding to the back to cover the machine stitching and slip-stitch in place. See Bias Binding on page 7 for complete directions.

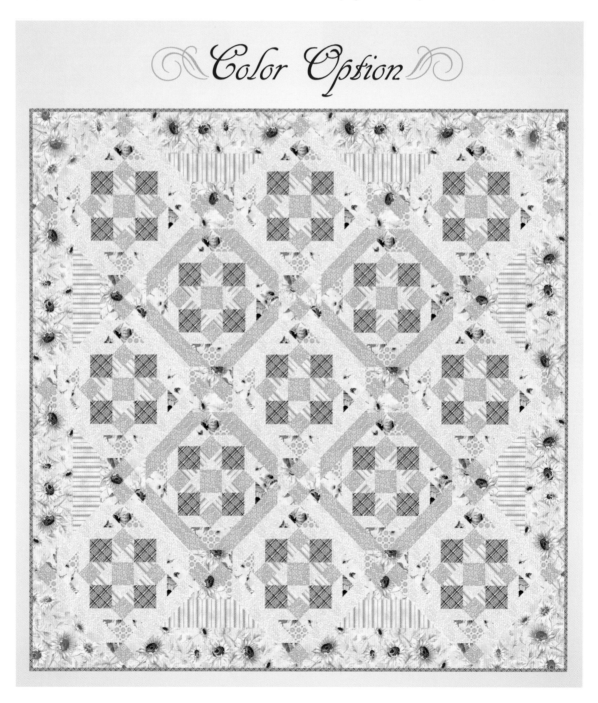

Color Option

Villa Sunset

Villa Breeze

This quilt makes the most of the focal fabric from the Full Sun Collection by WillowBerry Lane with Maywood Studio. There are two blocks, along with setting triangles for finishing the borders. Once you've used setting triangles in a quilt, you'll be looking for more quilt patterns that call for finishing "on point".

Fabrics & Supplies

Finished Size: 90" x 90" • Block Size: 16"

A—3-1/4 yards BLUE LARGE FLORAL
    All Blocks

B—2 yards GOLD/BLUE STRIPE
    Block 1

C—1-1/8 yards BLUE TONE-ON-TONE
    Block 1

D—1-1/8 yards BLUE FILIGREE
    Block 2

E—3/4 yard MEDIUM GOLD TONE-ON-TONE
    Block 2

F—3 yards BLUE FLORAL STRIPE
    Setting Triangles

Backing—8 yards BLUE LARGE FLORAL

Binding—1 yard BLUE TONE-ON-TONE

Optional—Folded Corner BerriAngles®
    100—3" Finished
    100—1" Finished

Note: *See Piggy-Back Method in BerriAngles®*
    section on page 11.

Before beginning this project,
see the General Instructions on pages 5-7.

Cutting Instructions

Block 1 & 2

Make 25 Blocks

Note: *If your Fabric E measures at least 40-1/2" wide,*
    you will only need to cut (4) 4-1/2" wide strips for
    the 4-1/2" (E-1) squares.

Fabric A BLUE LARGE FLORAL:
    Cut (9) 12-1/2" x 40" strips.
        From the strips cut:
        (25) 12-1/2" center squares   (A-1)

Fabric B GOLD/BLUE STRIPE:
    Cut (27) 2-1/2"x 40" strips.
        From the strips cut:
        (32) 2-1/2" x 12-1/2" border strips (B-1)
        (32) 2-1/2" x 16-1/2" border strips (B-2)

Fabric C BLUE TONE-ON-TONE:
    Cut (8) 4-1/2" x 40" strips.
        From the strips cut:
        (64) 4-1/2" squares   (C-1)

Fabric D BLUE FILIGREE:
    Cut (15) 2-1/2" x 40" strips.
        From the strips cut:
        (18) 2-12" x 12-1/2" border strips (D-1)
        (18) 2-1/2" x 16-1/2" border strips (D-2)

Fabric E MEDIUM GOLD TONE-ON-TONE:
    Cut (5) 4-1/2" x 40" strips.
        From the strips cut:
        (36) 4-1/2" squares   (E-1)

Piecing Block 1

Make 16 Blocks

1. Stitch 2-1/2" x 12-1/2" GOLD/BLUE STRIPE (B-1) border strips to opposite sides of (16) 12-1/2" BLUE LARGE FLORAL (A-1) center squares. Press seams toward border. Stitch 2-1/2" x 16-1/2" GOLD/BLUE STRIPE (B-2) border strips to the remaining sides of the center squares. Blocks will measure 16-1/2".

2. Draw a diagonal line across the wrong side of the 4-1/2" BLUE TONE-ON-TONE (C-1) squares. With right sides together, place the 4-1/2" squares on each corner of the (16) Block 1. Stitch on the drawn line. Press toward the outside corner. Trim away excess fabric. Block 1 measures 16-1/2" square.

Piecing Block 2

Make Nine Blocks

1. Stitch 2-1/2" x 12-1/2" BLUE FILIGREE (D-1) border strips to opposite sides of nine 12-1/2" BLUE LARGE FLORAL (A-1) center squares. Press seams toward border. Stitch 2-1/2" x 16-1/2" BLUE FILIGREE (D-2) border strips to the remaining sides of the center squares. Blocks will measure 16-1/2".

2. Draw a diagonal line across the wrong side of the 4-1/2" MEDIUM GOLD TONE-ON-TONE (E-1) squares. With right sides together, place the 4-1/2" squares on each corner of the nine Block 2. Stitch on the drawn line. Press toward the outside corner. Trim away excess fabric. Block 2 measures 16-1/2" square.

Quilt Top Cutting Instructions

Fabric F BLUE FLORAL STRIPE:

Cut (3) 12" x 108" lengthwise strips with the wide flower band at the bottom of each strip as shown.

12"

1. Cut twelve setting triangles from the strips using a ruler with a 45-degree marking, taking care to cut the triangles with the wide floral band at the bottom.

Make 12

Note: *You will only use the triangles with the wide floral band at the bottom for the quilt. Save the unused triangles to make pillows.*

2. Layout sixteen Block 1, nine Block 2, and twelve setting triangles on a large flat surface as shown. Sew the blocks and setting triangles together in diagonal rows. Press seams toward the setting triangles and Block 2.

Note: *When joining a setting triangle to a block, align the fabrics at one edge and let the triangle extend beyond the opposite edge of the block, as shown below.*

3. Sew the rows together, matching seams and pinning for best results. Press all row seams in one direction. Trim the quilt edges to allow for a 1/4" seam allowance.

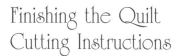

Finishing the Quilt
Cutting Instructions

Backing Fabric - BLUE LARGE FLORAL:
    Cut (3) 96" x Full Width of Fabric rectangles.

Binding Fabric - BLUE TONE-ON-TONE:
    Cut enough 2-1/4"-wide bias strips to
    make a 410" long strip.

1. Trim the selvages from the edges of the backing
   rectangles. Sew the long edges of the rectangles together,
   using a 1/2" seam allowance. Press the seams open.

2. Layer the pieced backing, batting, and quilt top. Baste
   the layers together and machine- or hand-quilt as
   desired. See page 5 in the General Instructions for
   more information.

3. Prepare the binding and sew to the quilt front using a 1/4"
   seam allowance. Fold the binding to the back to cover the
   machine stitching and slip-stitch in place. Sew Bias
   Binding on page 7 for complete directions.

Villa Breeze

Color Options

Breezy Pillow Shams

These standard pillow shams are a breeze to piece. You'll love the way they look when paired with the Villa Breeze quilt.

Fabrics & Supplies

Finished size: 38-1/2" x 29-1/2"

Note: *Yardage and Cutting Instructions are for two shams. Repeat sewing instructions to make a second sham.*

A—1-1/4 yards BLUE/ECRU STRIPE
    Front Center

B—3/4 yard BLUE FILIGREE
    Front Center

C—1-1/4 yards BLUE LARGE FLORAL
    Border

Backing—2-1/2 yards BLUE LARGE FLORAL

Sham back—5-1/8 yards SMALL BLUE FLORAL

Binding—3/4 yard BLUE/ECRU STRIPE

Batting—(2) 44" x 35" rectangles

Before beginning this project,
see General Instructions on pages 5-7.

Cutting Instructions

Breezy Sham Front

Note: *If your Fabric B measures at least 41" wide, you will only need to cut (1) 5-1/2" wide strip for the B-1 rectangles. If your Fabric C measures at least 41" wide, you will only need to cut (6) 5" wide strips for the C-1 and C-2 rectangles.*

Fabric A BLUE/ECRU STRIPE:
    Cut (2) 20-1/2" x 40" strips.
        From the strips cut:
        (4) 20-1/2" x 12-1/2" side rectangles(A-1)

Fabric B BLUE FILIGREE:
    Cut (2) 5-1/2" x 40" strips.
        From the strips cut:
        (2) 5-1/2" x 20-1/2" center rectangles(B-1)
    (8) 1" x 40" strips.
        From the strips cut:
        (4) 1" x 20-1/2" trim strips   (B-2)
        (4) 1" x 29-1/2" trim strips   (B-3)

Fabric C BLUE LARGE FLORAL:
    Cut (8) 5" x 40" strips.
        From the strips cut:
        (4) 5" x 20-1/2" border strips   (C-1)
        (4) 5" x 38-1/2" border strips   (C-2)

Piecing the Sham Front

1. Sew a 20-1/2" x 12-1/2" BLUE/ECRU STRIPE (A-1) side rectangle to each long edge of the 5-1/2" x 20-1/2" BLUE FILIGREE (B-1) center rectangle for the sham center. Press seams toward the center rectangle.

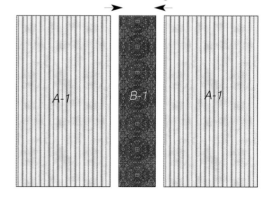

2. With wrong sides together, fold two 1" x 20-1/2" BLUE FILIGREE (B-2) trim strips in half lengthwise to measure

1/2" wide; press. Place strips on the right side of the pieced sham center from Step 1, aligning the raw edges of the strips with the 20-1/2" edges of the front. Baste in place. Repeat with two 1" x 29-1/2" BLUE FILIGREE (B-3) trim strips, placing them on the 29-1/2" edges of the sham center.

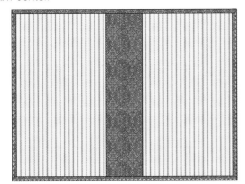

3. Sew a 5" x 20-1/2" BLUE LARGE FLORAL (C-1) border strip to the side edges of the sham center. Press seams toward the strips. Sew a 5" x 38-1/2" BLUE LARGE FLORAL (C-2) border strip to the top and bottom edges of the sham center. Press seams toward the strips.

Finishing the Sham
Cutting Instructions

Backing BLUE LARGE FLORAL:
  Cut (2) 44" x 35" backing rectangles.

Sham Back SMALL BLUE FLORAL:
  Cut (4) 42-1/2" x 29-1/2" rectangles.

Binding BLUE/ECRU STRIPE:
  Cut enough 2-3/8"-wide bias strips
  to make two 160" long strips.

1. Smooth a SMALL BLUE FLORAL backing rectangle, right side down, on a flat surface. Center batting on backing rectangle and then the pieced sham front, right side up, on batting. Baste the layers together and machine- or hand-quilt as desired.

2. Trim any excess batting and backing even with the raw edge of the pieced sham front, allowing for a 1/4" seam allowance.

3. Fold two of the 42-1/2" x 29-1/2" SMALL BLUE FLORAL rectangles in half with wrong sides facing, aligning the 29-1/2" edges opposite the fold; press. The back rectangles measure 21-1/4" x 29-1/2".

4. Smooth the quilted sham front, right side down, on a flat surface. Position a back rectangle on one half of the front, aligning three edges with the fold near the center. Position the second back rectangle over the remaining half of the front in the same manner. The rectangles will overlap approximately 4". Baste the layers together 1/4" from the raw edges.

5. To create the flange, sew through all layers, stitching-in-the-ditch on the seam that joins the BLUE LARGE FLORAL border to the sham center.

6. Prepare the binding and sew to the sham front using a 1/4" seam allowance. Fold the binding to the back to cover the machine stitching and slip-stitch in place. See Bias Binding on page 7 for complete directions.

Color Option

117

Breezy Pillow Cover

Fabrics & Supplies

Finished size: 21-1/2" x 21-1/2"

A—Fat Eighth of BLUE FILIGREE
    Block

B—Fat Quarter of GOLD TONE-ON-TONE
    Block

C—Fat Eighth of BLUE TONE-ON-TONE
    Block

D—3/4 yard BLUE FLORAL STRIPE
    Border

Backing—3/4 yard BLUE LARGE FLORAL

Cover back—1-1/4 yards BLUE FILIGREE

Binding—1/2 yard BLUE FILIGREE

Batting—27" square

Optional—Half-Square BerriAngles®
    12—3" Finished

Before beginning this project,
see the General Instructions on pages 5-7.

Cutting Instructions

Breezy Sham Front

Fabric A BLUE FILIGREE:
    Cut (2) 3-7/8" x 20" strips.   (A-1)

Fabric B GOLD TONE-ON-TONE:
    Cut (3) 3-7/8" x 20" strips.   (B-1)
    From one strip cut:
    (2) 3-7/8" squares   (B-2)

Fabric C BLUE TONE-ON-TONE:
    Cut (1) 3-7/8" x 20" strip.
    From the strip cut:
    (2) 3-7/8" squares   (C-1)
    Cut (1) 3-1/2" square.   (C-2)

Fabric D BLUE FLORAL STRIPE:
    Cut (4) 3-3/4" x 24" lengthwise
    border strips, centering
    flowers in each strip as shown.   (D-1)

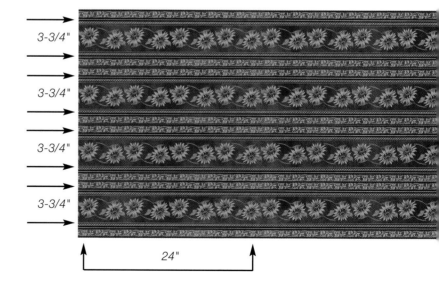

3-3/4"

3-3/4"

3-3/4"

3-3/4"

24"

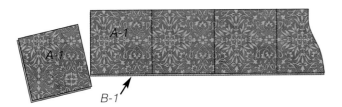

Piecing the Center Block

1. With right sides together, layer the 3-7/8" BLUE FILIGREE (A-1) strips and GOLD TONE-ON-TONE (B-1) strips in pairs; press. Cut the layered strips into (10) 3-7/8" squares.

2. Keeping the above squares together in pairs, use a 3" Finished Half-Square BerriAngles® or draw a diagonal line across the wrong side of all the GOLD TONE-ON-TONE (B-1) squares. Stitch 1/4" on both sides of the drawn line. Cut apart on the drawn line; press seams toward the dark triangle. The HALF-SQUARE TRIANGLES MEASURE 3-1/2" square. Make 20 HALF-SQUARE TRIANGLES.

Make 20

3. Repeat Step 2 to make four HALF-SQUARE TRIANGLES with the GOLD TONE-ON-TONE (B-2) squares and BLUE TONE-ON-TONE (C-1) squares.

4. Layout the HALF-SQUARE TRIANGLES from Steps 2 and 3 and the BLUE TONE-ON-TONE (C-2) square as shown.

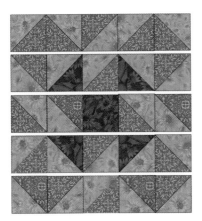

5. Sew the pieces together in rows. Press the seam allowances in one direction, alternating the direction from row to row. Sew the rows together; press. The block measures 15-1/2" square.

Adding the Border

1. Center and sew a 3-3/4" x 24" BLUE FLORAL STRIPE (D-1) border strip along one edge of the center block, starting and stopping the stitching 1/4" from the corners of the block. Attach a border strip to each edge of the block in the same manner.

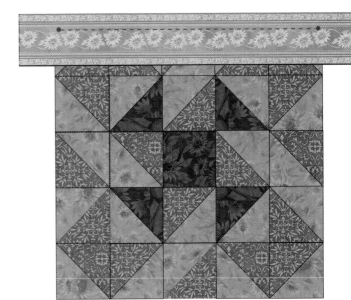

2. To miter the corners, place pillow cover right side down. Fold one border strip over the adjacent strip so they are laying flat. Use a ruler and pencil to draw a 45-degree stitching line from the point where the strips meet to the point where the stitching ends. Fold the pillow cover diagonally so the edges of the two border strips line up with right sides together.

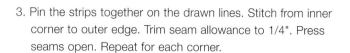

3. Pin the strips together on the drawn lines. Stitch from inner corner to outer edge. Trim seam allowance to 1/4". Press seams open. Repeat for each corner.

Finishing the Pillow Cover Cutting Instructions

Backing BLUE LARGE FLORAL:
   Cut (1) 27" backing square.

Cover Back BLUE FILIGREE:
   Cut (2) 25-1/2" x 21-1/2" rectangles.

Binding BLUE FILIGREE:
   Cut enough 2-1/2"-wide bias strips
   to make 100" long strip.

Finishing the Pillow Cover

1. Smooth a BLUE LARGE FLORAL backing square, right side down, on a flat surface. Center batting on backing rectangle and then the pieced pillow cover front, right side up, on batting. Baste the layers together and machine- or hand-quilt as desired.

2. Trim any excess batting and backing even with the raw edge of the pieced pillow cover front, allowing for a 1/4" seam allowance.

3. Fold the 25-1/2" x 21-1/2" rectangles in half with wrong sides facing, aligning the 21-1/2" edges opposite the fold; press. The back rectangles measure 12-3/4" x 21-1/2".

4. Smooth the quilted pillow cover front, right side down, on a flat surface. Position a back rectangle on one half of the front, aligning three edges with the fold near the center. Position the second back rectangle over the remaining half of the front in the same manner. The rectangles will overlap approximately 4". Baste the layers together 1/4" from the raw edges.

5. Prepare the binding and sew to the pillow cover front using a 1/4" seam allowance. Fold the binding to the back to cover the machine stitching and slip-stitch in place. See Bias Binding on page 7 for complete directions.

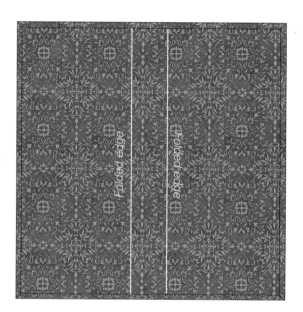

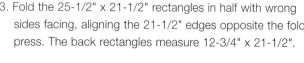

Button Pillow Cover

This cute button pillow will add personality to any room in your home.

Cutting Instructions

Fabric A BLUE FLORAL STRIPE:
  Cut (2) 12" x 50" lengthwise strips with the wide
    flower band at the top of each strip as shown.

12"

Piecing the Front

1. Cut two triangles from each strip using a ruler with a
   45-degree marking, taking care to cut the triangles with
   the wide floral band at the top.

Fabrics & Supplies

Finished size: 22" x 22"

A—1-7/8 yards BLUE FLORAL STRIPE
        Front, Trim, and Button

Backing—3/4 yard BLUE LARGE FLORAL

Cover back—1-1/3 yards BLUE LARGE FLORAL

Binding—1/2 yard BLUE FILIGREE

Batting—26" square

1-1/2" metal button to cover

Before beginning this project,
see the General Instructions on pages 5-7.

Note: *If you made the Villa Breeze Quilt,
  make this pillow with the unused triangles from that quilt.*

*Note: You will only use the triangles with the wide floral band at
  the top for the pillow cover.*

2. Sew triangles together in pairs. Press seams in opposite directions. Join the pairs. Press seams in one direction.

Finishing the Pillow Cover
Cutting Instructions

Fabric A BLUE FLORAL STRIPE:
  Cut (1) 3-3/4" x 66" trim strip,
      centering a narrow flower band in strip.

Backing Fabric - BLUE LARGE FLORAL:
  Cut (1) 26" backing square.

Cover Back Fabric - BLUE LARGE FLORAL:
  Cut (2) 26" x 23" rectangles.

Binding Fabric - BLUE FILIGREE:
  Cut enough 2-1/2"-wide bias strips to
      make a 100" long strip.

Finishing the Pillow Cover

1. Smooth BLUE LARGE FLORAL backing square, right side down, on a flat surface. Center batting on backing rectangle and then the pieced pillow cover front, right side up, on batting. Baste the layers together and machine- or hand-quilt as desired.

2. Trim any excess batting and backing even with the raw edge of the pieced pillow cover front, allowing for a 1/4" seam allowance.

3. With right sides together, fold the 3-3/4" x 66" BLUE FLORAL STRIPE strip in half to align the long edges. Sew the long edges together, forming a tube. Turn the tube

right side out. Press, centering the seam on the back. Cut in half to make two trim tubes.

4. Position the tubes from Step 3 on the quilted pillow cover front so they cross at the center and the ends are centered over the corners as shown. Edge-stitch the tubes in place. Trim the tubes even with the edges of the front.

5. Fold the 26" x 23" rectangles in half with wrong sides facing, aligning the 23" edges opposite the fold; press. The back rectangles measure 13" x 23".

6. Smooth the quilted pillow cover front, right side down, on a flat surface. Position a back rectangle on one half of the front, aligning three edges with the fold near the center. Position the second back rectangle over the remaining half of the front in the same manner. The rectangles will overlap approximately 3". Baste the layers together 1/4" from the raw edges.

7. Prepare the binding and sew to the pillow cover front using a 1/4" seam allowance. Fold the binding to the back to cover the machine stitching and slip-stitch in place. See Bias Binding on page 7 for complete directions.

8. To cover the button, place the 1-1/2" metal button on the wrong side of a 3"-square scrap of BLUE FLORAL STRIPE. Draw a circle about 1/2" beyond the edge of the button. Place button on a batting scrap, draw around the button exactly at the button's edge. Cut out the fabric and batting circles on the lines. Center the batting circle on the wrong side of the fabric circle, then center the button on the batting. Refer to the package directions to complete the covered button. Sew button to the center front of pillow cover.

Villa Breeze

Button Pillow

Villa Shower Curtain

Bird-in-Air blocks and scrappy triangles make this garden inspired shower curtain a wonderful enhancement for your master bath. This shower curtain coordinates with the Villa Garden Queen Bedroom ensemble to create a master suite that embodies elegance and romance.

Fabrics & Supplies

Finished size: 70" x 72"

A—1 yard ECRU TINY FLORAL
    All Blocks

B—1 yard each of FOUR MEDIUM GREEN PRINTS
    All Blocks

C—1/2 yard GREEN LARGE FLORAL
    Bird-in-Air Blocks

D—1/2 yard GREEN POLKA DOT

E—2-1/2 yards ECRU/GREEN STRIPE
    Stripe Panels

F—1/4 yard GREEN TONE-ON-TONE
    Narrow Border

Backing—4-1/4 yards ECRU/GREEN STRIPE

Binding—7/8 yard ECRU/GREEN STRIPE

Batting—76" x 78" rectangle

Optional—Half-Square BerriAngles®
    84—2-1/2" Finished

Before beginning this project,
see General Instructions on pages 5-7.

Cutting Instructions

Bird-In-Air Block
Make 84 Blocks

Fabric A ECRU TINY FLORAL:
    Cut (8) 3-3/8" x 40" strips.   (A-1)

Fabric B FOUR MEDIUM GREEN PRINTS:
    Cut (2) 3-3/8" x 40" strips
        from each print to total 8 strips.   (B-1)
    (2) 3" x 40" strips from each print to total 8 strips.
        From the strips cut:
        (21) 3" squares to total 84 squares   (B-2)

Fabric C GREEN LARGE FLORAL:
    Cut (4) 3" x 40" strips.
        From the strips cut:
        (42) 3" squares   (C-1)

Fabric D GREEN POLKA DOT:
    Cut (4) 3" x 40" strips.
        From the strips cut:
        (42) 3" squares   (D-1)

Piecing the Bird-in-Air Block

1. With right sides together, layer the 3-3/8" x 40" ECRU TINY FLORAL (A-1) and MEDIUM GREEN PRINT (B-1) strips in pairs for a total of eight pairs; press. Cut the layered pairs into 3-3/8" squares, cutting (21) 3-3/8" squares from each of the four ECRU TINY FLORAL/MEDIUM GREEN PRINTS fabric combinations.

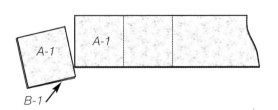

2. Keeping the above squares together in pairs, use a 2-1/2" Finished Half-Square BerriAngles® or draw a diagonal line across the wrong side of all the ECRU TINY FLORAL (A-1) squares. Stitch 1/4" on both sides of the drawn line. Cut apart on the drawn line; press seams toward the dark triangle. The HALF-SQUARE TRIANGLES measure 3" square. Make 42 HALF-SQUARE TRIANGLES from each MEDIUM GREEN PRINT for a total of 168.

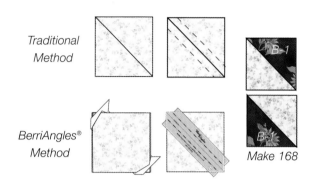

Traditional Method

BerriAngles® Method

Make 168

3. Arrange one 3" MEDIUM GREEN PRINT (B-2) square, one 3" LARGE GREEN FLORAL (C-1) square, and two HALF-SQUARE TRIANGLES with different greens (made in Step 2). Sew the squares and half-square triangles together in pairs; press seams toward the squares. Sew the pairs together; press. The BIRD–IN-AIR block measures 5-1/2" square. Make 42.

Make 42

4. Arrange one 3" MEDIUM GREEN PRINT (B-2) square, one 3" GREEN POLKA DOT (D-1) square, and two HALF-SQUARE TRIANGLES with different greens (made in Step 2). Sew the squares and half-square triangles together in pairs; press seams toward the squares. Sew the pairs together; press. The BIRD-IN-AIR block measures 5-1/2" square. Make 42.

Make 42

Cutting Instructions

Pieced Panel
Make Three Panels

Fabric A ECRU TINY FLORAL:
Cut (1) 4-1/2" x 40" strip.
From the strip cut: (6) 4-1/2" squares; cut each in half diagonally to make twelve triangles.　　　(A-2)

Fabric B FOUR MEDIUM GREEN PRINTS:
Cut (1) 8-3/8" x 40" strip from each print to total 4 strips. From each strip cut: (3) 8-3/8" squares; cut each into quarters diagonally to make 12 triangles of each print, 48 total.　(B-3)
(1) 4-1/2" x 40" strip from each print to total 4 strips. From each strip cut: (3) 4-1/2" squares; cut each in half diagonally to make 6 triangles of each print, 24 total.　(B-4)

Piecing the Panels

1. Sew together an ECRU TINY FLORAL (A-2) triangle and a MEDIUM GREEN PRINT (B-4) triangle. Press seam toward the dark triangle. Make twelve pieced triangles.

Make 12

2. Lay out 28 BIRD-IN-AIR blocks, 14 MEDIUM GREEN PRINT (B-3) triangles, four pieced triangles from Step 1, and two MEDIUM GREEN PRINT (B-4) triangles on a large flat surface as shown. Sew the blocks and triangles together in diagonal rows. Press rows in alternating directions. Sew the rows together; press. The pieced panel measures approximately 18" x 53". Make 3 panels. There are 6 extra B-3 and B-4 triangles.

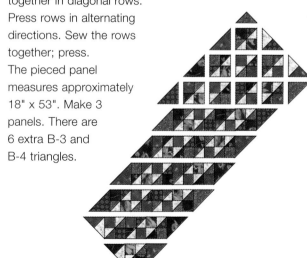

Cutting Instructions

Shower Curtain Top

Fabric E ECRU/GREEN STRIPE:
    Cut (2) 10-1/2" x 54" lengthwise strips.   (E-1)
    (4) 8-1/4 x 40" strips.   (E-2)

Fabric F GREEN TONE-ON-TONE:
    Cut (4) 1-1/2" x 40" strips.   (F-1)

Piecing the Shower Curtain Top

1. Measure the length of the pieced panels. Trim the 10-1/2" x 54" ECRU/GREEN STRIPE (E-1) strips to this length.

2. Sew together the long edges of the three pieced panels and two trimmed ECRU/GREEN STRIPE (E-1) strips to complete the center section. Press seams toward the strips.

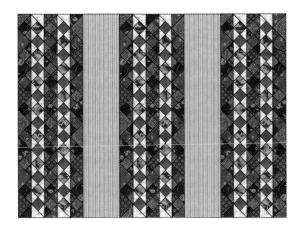

3. Trim the selvages from the four 1-1/2" x 40" GREEN TONE-ON-TONE (F-1) strips. Sew the strips together in pairs to make two long strips; press.

4. Trim the selvages from the four 8-1/4" x 40" ECRU/GREEN STRIPE (E-2) strips. Sew the strips together in pairs to make two long strips; press.

5. Measure the width of the center section. Use this measurement to trim the GREEN TONE-ON-TONE (F-1) strips from Step 3 and the ECRU/GREEN STRIPE (E-2) strips from Step 4. Sew the trimmed strips to the top and bottom edges of the center section as shown. Press seams away from the center section. The shower curtain measures approximately 72" x 70".

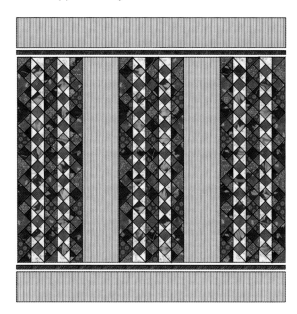

Finishing the Shower Curtain
Cutting Instructions

Backing Fabric ECRU/GREEN STRIPE:
    Cut (2) 76-1/2" x Full Width of Fabric rectangles

Binding Fabric ECRU/GREEN STRIPE:
    Cut enough 2-1/4"-wide bias strips
    to make a 300" long strip.

1. Trim the selvages from the edges of the backing rectangles. Sew the long edges of the rectangles together, using a 1/2" seam allowance. Press the seam open.

2. Layer the pieced backing, batting, and shower curtain top. Baste the layers together and machine- or hand-quilt as desired. See page 5 in the General Instructions for more information.

3. Prepare the binding and sew to the curtain front using a 1/4" seam allowance. Fold the binding to the back to cover the machine stitching and slip-stitch in place. See Bias Binding on page 7 for complete directions.

4. Hang shower curtain with shower curtain rings or make buttonholes along the top of the curtain, using a shower liner as a template for buttonhole placement. Mark the position with a water-soluble pen; make buttonholes at the marks.

Color Options
Shower Curtain

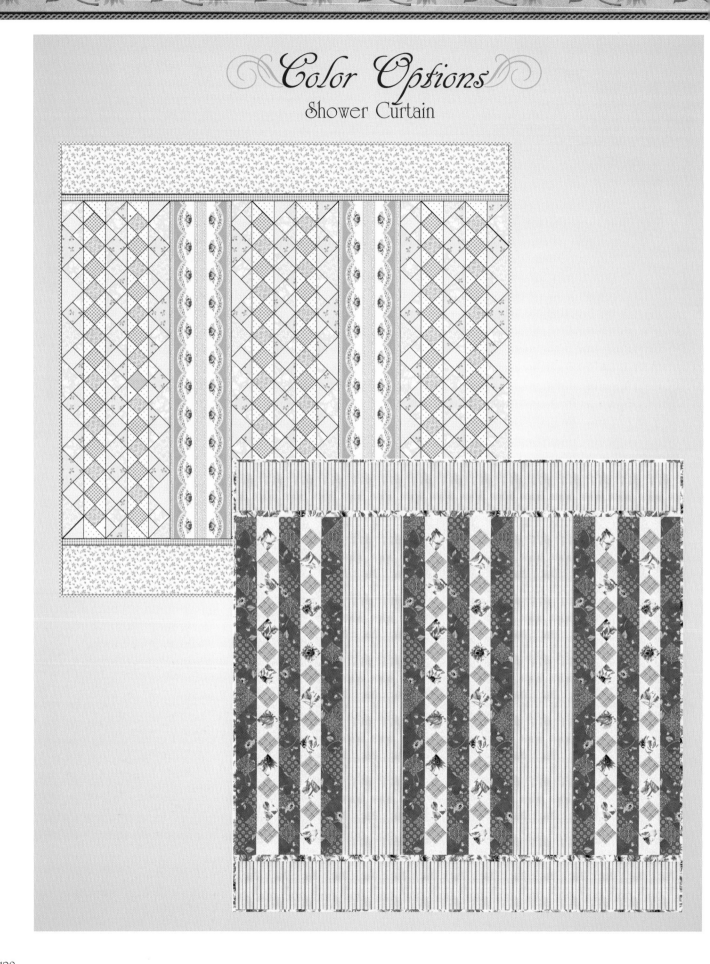